A DASH OF
MUSTARD

>>>>>>>> <<<<<<<<

A DASH OF MUSTARD

Mustard in the Kitchen & on the Table:
»>«< *Recipes & Traditions* »>«<

KATY HOLDER AND JANE NEWDICK
WITH EXTRA MATERIAL BY IAN WISNIEWSKI

FIREFLY BOOKS

A FIREFLY BOOK

First published in Canada in 1996 by
Firefly Books Ltd
3680 Victoria Park Avenue
Willowdale, Ontario M2H 3K1

Canadian Cataloguing in Publication Data

Holder, Kathy
A dash of mustard: mustard in the kitchen and on the table

ISBN 1-55209-049-3

1. Mustard (Condiment). I. Newdick, Jane. II. Title.

TX819.M87H65 1996   641.6 384   C96-931053-6

This book was designed and produced by
Quarto Publishing plc
The Old Brewery
6 Blundell Street
London N7 9BH

Art Director: Moira Clinch
Design: Design Revolution
Senior Art Editor: Liz Brown
Copy Editors: Jackie Matthews and Fiona Hunter
Home Economist: Kathy Holder
Picture Researcher: Susannah Jayes
Picture Manager: Giulia Hetherington
Senior Editor: Sian Parkhouse
Editorial Director: Mark Dartford
Photographer: Philip Wilkins
Illustrator: Rodney Shackell

Typeset in Great Britain by Central Southern Typesetters, Eastbourne
Manufactured in Hong Kong by Regent Publishing Services Ltd
Printed in China by Leefung-Asco Printers Ltd

CONTENTS

—— ❯❯❮❮ ——

INTRODUCTION

MUSTARD IS A SIMPLE, EVERYDAY KIND OF SPICE, STRONG BUT FAMILIAR. IT HAS ALWAYS HAD AN IMPORTANT BUT UNDERSTATED ROLE IN THE KITCHEN, AND AT ONE TIME THE SICKROOM, TOO, THOUGH IT WAS SOMETIMES OVERLOOKED IN FAVOR OF RARER AND MORE EXOTIC SPICES. A REAL STALWART IN MANY CUISINES, MUSTARD ADDS HEAT AND PUNGENCY, SUBTLE FLAVOR, AND BRILLIANT COLOR TO PLAIN OR ELABORATE MEALS.

Perhaps because it has always been an easy plant to cultivate and is grown more or less ubiquitously throughout the world, the small creamy yellow or brown seeds of mustard have often been taken for granted as an ingredient and spice. Throughout its long history, mustard has been a flavoring which has sometimes been used carelessly or indis-criminately in the kitchen, gaining a reputation for heat with no subtlety which is very unfair. Mustard deserves better than this, as we set out to prove here through history, anecdote, myth, and inspiration.

The seeds of the mustard plant have been used as a spice, a condiment, and a medicine for as long as it is possible to trace, with evidence that early civilizations living along the Indus valley around 2,300 B.C. – and even earlier – seasoned their meat with it.

Mustard seed comes from a small annual plant of the *cruciferae* family, and there are three important types: white, black, and brown. The colors refer to the color of the ripened seed, not the flowers, which are all bright yellow. White mustard (*brassica alba*) is naturalized throughout northern Europe and North America, while black mustard (*brassica nigra*) is native to southern Europe and temperate western Asia. Brown mustard (*brassica juncea*) is native to India. The mustards are part of a vast plant family which includes all the cabbages and broccolis, radish and watercress, as well as

A field of mustard in full bloom is a memorable sight on a sunny day, with the vivid yellow of the flowers contrasting with a deep blue sky.

A manuscript illustration of a Flemish feast from the fourteenth century. Without doubt, mustard in some form would have been included in several of the dishes.

An elegant silver mustard pot, which would enhance any table setting.

non-edible varieties such as wallflowers. None of these cruciferous plants is poisonous, and all have antiscorbutic properties (meaning that they purify the blood). The seeds have to be harvested when they are completely ripe, but before they have burst from their little pea-shaped pods. Because black mustard seeds are hard to harvest – and is a process best done painstakingly by hand harvesting, brown mustard has now taken over from the black variety in commercial production, as it can be harvested economically on a large scale, using machines.

Mustard seeds when crushed produce an oil which is fierce and pungent. Used externally, this oil first irritates, then partially anesthetizes the sensory nerves, and so it has been used for centuries to relieve the symptoms of rheumatism, gout and arthritis, as well as colds and fever. Taken internally in large quantities, mustard oil is a powerful emetic, but used in smaller doses it has the effect of a digestive and diuretic, and also a stimulant. Other remedies incorporating mustard include chewing the seeds to relieve toothache and gargling for a sore throat with an infusion of

Mustard seeds, the most commonly used part of the plant.

mustard and warm wine. Mustard footbaths were a popular everyday treatment until quite recently, and mustard baths for the whole body have been in and out of fashion over the centuries. Poultices have definitely gone out of vogue, but these messy "bandages" were regularly prescribed for all manner of ailments at one time and often included mustard in their list of ingredients.

EARLY USES

In medieval times mustard was often used in cooking as a palliative to make old or badly preserved meat and dried fish edible by masking strong or rancid flavors. Its name in English suggests how it was used, as *must* is Anglo-Saxon for unfermented grape juice, with which it was commonly mixed, and *ardens* means hot or fiery. The seeds were used whole or roughly crushed in early times, as the dry mustard powder with which we are all familiar was not invented until late in the spice's history.

Every culture and country tends to have their mustard specialties and often towns or areas in each country where mustard production and processing is centered. French mustard, for example, is synonymous with the name Dijon – the town where the highly important French mustard industry is based. The French version is flavorful and sometimes grainy and mixed with wine vinegars, while Americans love a sweet, plastic variety squeezed straight from a bottle onto hot dogs and burgers. Because of its versatility and availability, mustard is often used in many cuisines as just one of many varied flavorings in a dish, but it also has specific uses. It is often used simply to add heat, which it does in many cases in Indian and Japanese food, and is also commonly used as an ingredient for pickling. At one time it was a

7

Brassica sinapsis, or wild mustard, is also called charlock. A field that seems to be clear of this weed can be plowed up after several years and quickly become a complete mass of yellow flowers.

cheaper way of adding ferocious heat than costly black pepper, and of course it was around before the arrival of chilies in Europe. It can also be used to give its own subtle flavor: for example, in recipes for mustard sauces which are often designed to be used with specific foods like oily fish. Think of mackerel with mustard sauce, or the Italian *mostarde e frutta candita* served with boiled meats. But often mustard really shines in its less obvious uses as catalyst and enhancer to other ingredients. What mayonnaise or vinaigrette dressing would be worth eating without a little mustard to help the emulsion along, and how much less piquant would many cheese dishes be without a pinch of the magical paste or powder?

Dijon, the French mustard city

It was the Romans who first introduced mustard to France (or Gaul, as it then was) and the French took to it wholeheartedly. The center of the French mustard industry has always been Dijon in Burgundy, the wine and vinegar producing area. By the fourteenth century, the town's mustard makers had adopted their own commercial trademark from the motto of the Duke Philip the Bold: "Moult me Tarde," or "I ardently desire." Some people claim this was abbreviated into "moustarde" – hence the French name for the condiment. The Dijon style of mustard was a blend of mustard seed and grape must, although variations added honey, oil, and vinegar.

By the end of the fifteenth century, mustard was losing ground to other spices, and it remained in decline until the early eighteenth century, when a certain Monsieur Jean Naigeon invented a new recipe using verjuice instead of vinegar. The wine growers of Burgundy were happy to supply as much verjuice as was needed. It was a great success, and this period saw the beginnings of many of the great family companies with such well-known names as Maille and Grey Poupon. Dijon is still as important as ever to the French mustard industry and home to large companies such as SEGMA Liebeg Maille, which includes Maille, Grey Poupon, and Amora.

The winegrowers of Burgundy and the mustard makers of Dijon worked together to give the region a reputation for its mustard that endures today.

A fine collection of old ceramic mustard pots on display in Dijon, France.

THE PLANT

USUALLY PLANTED BETWEEN LATE FEBRUARY AND EARLY APRIL THROUGHOUT THE TEMPERATE WORLD, MUSTARD PLANTS NEED NO SPECIAL CARE TO FLOURISH. THEIR FAMILIAR BRIGHT YELLOW FLOWERS PROVIDE SPLASHES OF COLOR IN THE LANDSCAPE.

Brown mustard,
Brassica juncea.
The plant has vigorous and plentiful leaves, while the flower stems are smaller with more delicate and widely spaced flowers.

10

Mustard belongs to the *cruciferae* group of plants, a name which stems from the characteristic four petals of the flower which form the shape of a cross. All mustard varieties are annuals and easily grown from seed. The seed pods are harvested in the summer and early fall when ripe, but before they burst, scattering the seeds.

Three types of mustard plant are grown. These are *brassica nigra* (black mustard), *brassic juncea* (brown mustard), and *brassica alba*, sometimes called *brassica hirta* or *sinapis alba* (white mustard). These names, stemming from the color of the seeds, provide a handy color coding. Black mustard seeds, with their dark rusty color, are the smallest of the three types, though the plant itself towers over the others, reaching a height of 10 feet or more.

Originally a native of southern Europe, the Middle East, and western Asia, black mustard used to be cultivated throughout Europe, and, since it yields the most flavor of all, was many producers' first choice. However, what it offers in terms of flavor it exacts in production. It can grow to be very tall, needs rich soil to thrive, and is brittle, which means the seeds can be released too easily. This makes commercial mechanical harvesting very difficult. So black mustard has become the preserve of peasant farmers who can harvest by hand in places such

White mustard,
Brassica alba.
The bright yellow flowers slowly open up the length of the stem, and the pods set seed in sequence. The seed pods are larger than those of the black mustard plant, hold about three seeds, and are covered in hairs.

as Sicily, Ethiopia, the CIS, and India.

Brown mustard production has stepped in to take the place of black since it can be harvested mechanically. The plants are shorter, growing up to about three feet – with paler yellow flowers than black, but the dark, reddish-brown seeds are larger than black ones, although less pungent. It is native to Africa, India, China, and Pakistan.

White mustard, which is indigenous to the Mediterranean and central Europe, is now grown in most temperate climates worldwide, including the U.S.A., Canada, and Great Britain. As a plant it grows to about 2½ feet and flourishes in heavy or sandy loam. The seeds of white mustard are the largest of the three kinds, but have the mildest flavor.

A large field of mustard being cut with a horse-drawn reaper between the world wars in Britain. The cut plants have been gathered into small bundles and stood in stooks.

11

*B*lack mustard.
Brassica nigra
The leaves are large and coarse, but the seed pods are smooth and small and held close to the stems. The branching flower stems have small, narrow leaves, tapering to a point at each end.

A Canadian field of white mustard in full flower. Canada has become one of the largest growers of mustard seed, particularly since World War II, and is the world's largest exporter of the crop.

MUSTARD IN THE KITCHEN

*ALTHOUGH WE THINK FIRST OF THE SEEDS WHEN IT
COMES TO THE CULINARY USES OF MUSTARD, ALMOST ALL PARTS OF
THE PLANT CAN BE USED IN COOKING.*

A coarse-grain mustard, in which the seeds have been only lightly crushed, adds texture as well as flavour to a dish.

14

As a cooking ingredient, mustard has a more complex role than most simple spices. True, a pinch can be added to the cheese dish, for example, to add a little heat and a subtle flavor, but mustard is often used in a more considered way – as a crucial part of a recipe, not just a flavoring afterthought. It also has an important part to play as a thickener and, in the case of oil-based sauces or dressings, as an aid to emulsification. Like many other spices, it has a definite affinity with certain foods – think of mustard and herrings, or mustard and pork. This may have as much to do with the mustard acting as a digestive for these oily foods as it does to a happy marriage of two flavors. But there are other cases, where mustard and certain other ingredients – like tomatoes, or green beans – simply combine beautifully, and it is really quite hard to say why.

People have relished spicy heat in foods for centuries, with mustard reigning supreme as the provider of this stimulation until peppercorns became widely exported. Mustard adds more than heat, however its subtle flavor more than the fierceness which has really been explored in many classic dishes and combinations of food. In fact, cooking heat will reduce the pungency of mustard, leaving only the flavor; so if heat is required, mustard should be added near the end of the cooking time and the dish should then be simmered gently, for as short a time as possible.

To make mustard from powder to serve as a simple condiment with food, only cold water should ever be used – a point many people forget. The reason is this: on adding cold water to ground mustard seeds, a chemical reaction occurs between the enzyme myrosin and the glucosides sinigrin in black mustard seed, or sinalbin in white mustard seed. The water acts as a catalyst, allowing the myrosin to ferment the sinigrin producing the essential oil of mustard (allyl isothiocyanate), potassium salt, and sugar, which gives it a sharp taste and strong smell. The myrosin acts on the sinalbin to make sulfo-cyanate of acrinyl, sulfate or sinapine and sugar milder in taste and less aromatic. If hot water is used instead, the chemical reaction goes awry, leaving heat but also bitterness and a lack of flavor. All this science in the kitchen is therefore very important, but all you need to know is that to make the strong and distinctive taste of English mustard, *cold* water is essential. Always let mustard stand after mixing for ten minutes before eating it.

FLAVORS OF THE ORIENT

Whole mustard seeds can be coarsely ground and added to foods, or they can be used complete, in recipes such as pickled vegetables. Alternatively, they can be crushed with other spices for more complex seasonings to make eastern-inspired dishes, or toasted quickly until they start popping and added as a flavoring to some Indian dishes. Mustard oil is mainly used for cooking, mostly in certain Eastern recipes. White mustard leaves are eaten raw when young as salads, and when older can be cooked very briefly, as in a Chinese stir fry. Mustard powder is used to make mustard paste, usually mixed with water, and eaten as a relish with many foods, especially roast meats, served hot or cold, sautéed steaks, grilled fish, and many other, mainly protein-rich, foods. This is powerful stuff, generally eaten only in very small quantities. A pinch or two of dry mustard is useful when making mayonnaise or oil and vinegar dressing.

The younger leaves of the mustard plant have a distinctive taste which holds its own against strong dressings.

Mustard, with its many uses, would have been relied upon in the nineteenth-century kitchen as much as other staples, such as flour and eggs.

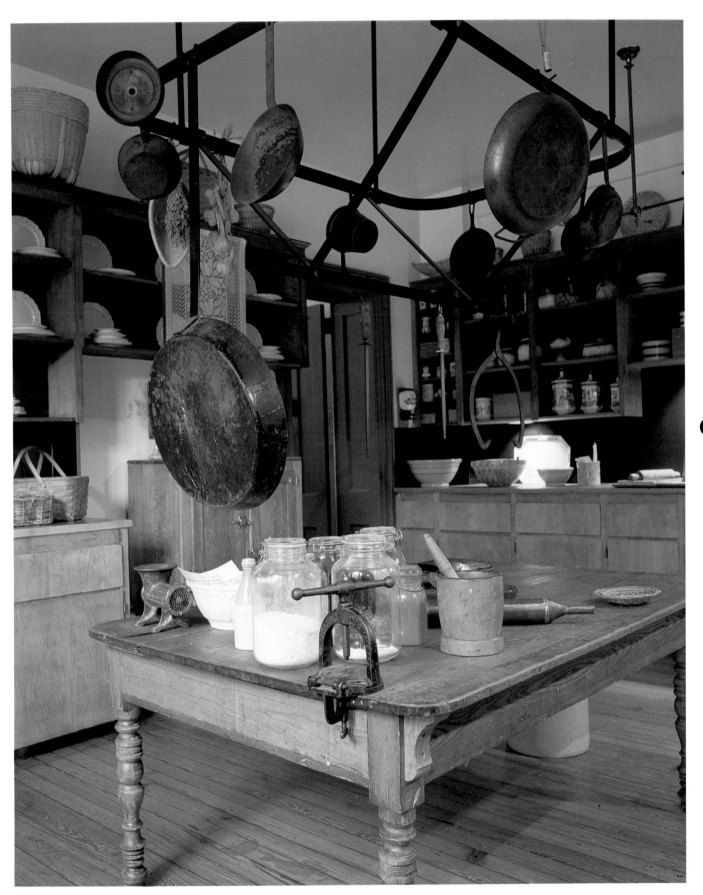

The Story of Mustard

Originally a weed growing unnoticed among cereal crops, mustard has been cultivated for its usefulness for at least 5,000 years. History is littered with references to it and recipes for cooking with it.

Fish formed a regular part of the Roman diet, as this fishing scene from a third-century B.C. Sicilian mosaic indicates. Recipes show that mustard was used frequently in a number of fish dishes.

In the early days, mustard leaves were eaten as a food as often as the seeds were used for flavoring. (The leaves are still eaten today, especially in Asian countries.) In the second century A.D., the Roman emperor Diocletian classified mustard as a food, not a condiment, perhaps for this reason. Nor is mustard described in the Bible as a condiment, but it is mentioned in the parable of the mustard seed (Mark 4), where Jesus compares the kingdom of God to a grain of mustard "which when it is sown in the earth, is less than all the seeds that be in the earth. But when it is sown, it groweth up, and becometh greater than all herbs, and shooteth out great branches; so that the fowls of the air may lodge under the shadow of it."

The earliest known cultivation and use of mustard was in India and China around 3000 B.C., where it was used to enliven a dull and monotonous diet of wheat and barley and some meats, cooked in sesame oil. By the time ancient Greek civilization was thriving, mustard was a common ingredient. It was often eaten in small handfuls and chewed with meat, producing a nutty flavor which also helped to mask less than perfect ingredients. The ancient Egyptians had also eaten mustard in this way.

The Greeks knew that mustard aided the digestion and had antiseptic properties: they used it in many different medicines and remedies, as well as in the kitchen. Both the ancient Greeks and the Romans had names for mustard which later came to inspire botanists to give the plant its scientific Latin name *sinapsis*.

From seed to paste

It was the Romans who began to realize the full potential of mustard by turning it into a paste with the addition of grape must (unfermented grape juice), vinegar, oil, and honey. Mustard was also used as a kind of pickling spice and preservative for meats, again often mixed with honey, salt, and vinegar. Crushed mustard seeds were sprinkled on all manner of dishes. The Romans had a passion for many different kinds of strongly flavored sauces, several of which included mustard. To our modern tastes they sound disgusting, relying as they did on rotted

Pliny the Elder (A.D. 33-79) outlined the medicinal uses of mustard in his Natural History, *which remained a key scientific work until the Renaissance.*

fish entrails and similar ingredients. *Liquamen* or *garum* was a salty fermented fish sauce, not unlike those found in Thailand, Vietnam, and Cambodia today. *Muria* was another, made with mustard and the brine drained from preserved tunafish.

Mustard was not universally popular in Rome, however – Plautus declared that "man fed on mustard could not be more sour and insensate." In his text written in the third century B.C., he actually condemned it as a "frightful poison." Apicius, the gourmand who lived through the reigns of Emperors Augustus and Tiberius, had no such qualms about any foods – he ate everything, with great enjoyment and in huge quantities. Apicius's party-throwing was renowned. When he had squandered all his money on feasts and fabulous meals, he decided life would no longer be worth living. He ordered one last banquet to end all banquets, included in which was one poisoned dish for him to eat and take his own life. He left behind the most comprehensive book on Roman cookery we have, called *De Re Coquinaria* (On Cookery).

The Byzantines added mustard to their food by way of sauces. They had several varieties, all of which relied on the seed as their crucial

---

≫≫≫ ≪≪≪

Catholic Tastes

His Holiness Pope John XXII reigned in Avignon from 1316 to 1334. He created the post of "grand moutardier du Pape" for his nephew, and was accused of nepotism for his pains.

≫≫≫ ≪≪≪

One for the Pot

King Louis XI of France (1423–83) carried his own personal pot of mustard, made for him by a Dijon mustard maker. He had a disconcerting habit of arriving unannounced to eat with his Parisian subjects, producing the mustard pot at each meal.

---

flavoring. An early type of vinaigrette was popular, eaten with many sorts of foods and liberally spiced with mustard. Another favorite was a sauce made from mustard and oxymel (a drink flavored with vinegar and honey).

THE POPE'S MUSTARD MAKER

The Romans are credited with bringing mustard to Gaul. There it was quickly taken up and successfully grown over the centuries, especially by the monks of St. Germain des Près in Paris and other holy orders, who, during the tenth century and afterward, became renowned for their skill in mustard making. It was a skill not limited to Paris by any means – by the thirteenth century, the Provost of Paris had also granted the vinegar makers of Dijon the right to make mustard, and the latter city was on the way to becoming the French capital of the condiment.

There is a saying in France that: "*Il se prend pour le moutardier du pape*" or "He thinks himself the Pope's mustard maker." It is applied to people who are vain, arrogant, and self-important. There are two versions of how the saying came about, the first one dating back to the time of Pope Clement VI. A member of the Medici family, Clement adored mustard

Charles VI of France had a weakness for mustard in all his food, especially a peasant dish consisting of herb-coated chicken with a mustard sauce. His personal cook was the famous Taillevent, who began his career as a kitchen porter in the early fourteenth century.

CHARLES·VI·ROY·DE·FRANCE

and ate it at every meal. Streams of people attempted to curry favor with the Pope by making delicious mustards for him. If there was one he really liked, the fortunate mustard maker would then receive many favors from the Pope. Those who were jealous would call the successful person "the Pope's mustard maker," particularly if they were prone to brag about their new honors. The second story relates how Pope John XXII (1316–34) had a ne'er-do-well nephew who was not even clever enough to become a cardinal (in those days an appointment often granted as a favor, unless

you were particularly stupid). The Pope therefore created a job for his nephew entitled "grand moutardier du pape" and ever afterward this expression has denoted someone who is stupid and conceited.

Mustard was a spice used in every French household, rich and poor. There is a story about King Charles VI who, during one of his campaigns against the English, found himself in the besieged town of Sainte-Menehoud. Here he called upon the hospitality of an ordinary peasant, who cooked him a dish of chicken grilled with herbs and a bread crumb coating, served with a mustard sauce. The king was delighted with this meal, and from then on this special dish was recreated for him wherever he wanted it by his chef, Taillevent. The king was so pleased with this chef that he was speedily elevated from kitchen porter to master of the king's kitchen. Taillevent went on to write what is now one of the oldest and most celebrated French cookery books, which gives a fascinating insight into the medieval world of food and includes recipes for such oddities as swan, heron, and peacock.

THE ALL-PURPOSE SPICE

In Britain, mustard was used as frequently in cooking as it was in France, being a very cheap spice and also native grown. Cultivated white mustard was probably a Roman introduction, judging by the seeds that have been found on old Roman sites such as Silchester. By the early medieval period, it had become a useful ingredient to relieve the monotony of pottage and salted meat, and in later centuries it was used in even greater quantity and in more inspiring ways. One record from 1418 describes the household of Dame Alicia de Breyene buying mustard for less than one farthing per pound. In one year, 84 pounds of it were eaten. We do not know how large her household was,

In the Middle Ages, poultry and meat joints would have been fatty and often tough. Slow cooking over a spit or in a large pot helped to counteract these drawbacks, as did the judicious addition of mustard.

but over one and a half pounds of mustard a week is a very large amount of spice! Mustard was usually made at home by crushing the seeds in a small quern, or mill, and then mixing them with water or vinegar, but it could also be bought from professional sauce makers or "mustarders." Mustard was essential eating with salt fish, particularly herrings and stockfish (dried and salted cod and similar fish). Another dish which always required mustard was brawn. Made from the head and fatty foreparts of a pig or boar, it invariably preceded other meats and fish at large meals. Popular from the thirteenth century until at least the seventeenth century, it featured in the feast to celebrate Neville's enthronement as Archbishop of Canterbury in 1467. The meal began with brawn and mustard served with malmsey (a sweet wine).

By the sixteenth century, the mustarders and sauce-makers had been joined by millers, who ground the mustard seed and sold it as a dry powder or a paste. One town in particular now became famous for its mustard production. Tewkesbury in Gloucestershire was a thriving wool town with plenty of other industry, too, such as tanning and leatherworking. Mustard making was chiefly a cottage industry carried out by the women of the town, who probably collected their own mustard seed from the

nearby fields and ground it in iron mortars – not with iron pestles, but with cannon balls. This coarse flour was mixed with pease flour and cinnamon, then moistened with a mixture of honey and vinegar (which had been infused with fiery horseradish root) and stirred for at least an hour. This stirring was thought to improve the mustard's texture and keeping qualities. The resultant paste was formed into balls the size of hens' eggs and then dried. The balls kept well, so could be sent across country. To reconstitute them, they were combined with water, vinegar, butter-milk, ale, cider – or indeed, whatever took your fancy. The horse-radish may have been the master stroke: Tewkesbury mustard became famous, and Thomas Tusser, author of *Five Hundred Points of Good Husbandry*

An illustration of King Charles VI's chef, Taillevent. He had great influence as a gastronome and cook until his death in 1395. Here he discusses fresh produce with a supplier of poultry.

The reputation of Tewkesbury mustard was confirmed in Shakespeare's Henry IV *part 1, in which Falstaff says of Poins that his wit was as "thick as Tewkesbury mustard." Today, however, mustard production in the town has completely died out.*

Dijon remains the mustard capital of France today, just as it was in the fourteenth century.

20

claimed in 1662, that "the best mustard is made in Tewkesbury. It is very wholesome in clearing the head." However, some people complained of the expense of this specialty. In 1639, one Peter Munday, being asked to pay three or four pence for a ball of the stuff, declared that he would prefer a farthing's worth of prepared mustard paste, which was "like the old dried thicke scurffe that sticks on the side of a mustard pot." The seventeenth century was the heyday of Tewkesbury mustard. Afterward it seemed to have waned in popularity, with the wild plants continuing to grow around the town as a poignant reminder of its former glory.

MUSTARD MANIA

The next interesting development in mustard took place in the early eighteenth century in Durham, aided by a Mrs. Clements. Mustard was still as popular as ever, and the spread of new tastes in food meant that there were always new ways to eat it. Moreover, many of the more exotic flavors and spices of the previous century were losing favor in place of simpler stalwarts such as mustard, herbs, and pickles. Around 1720, Mrs. Clements therefore devised a method of making very fine mustard flour without the oily mess usually produced when the

seed was ground too long. She put the seeds through several processes, rather like milling wheat, extracting any husk, and resulting in a smooth powder which was, apparently, mixed with cornstarch and turmeric. By 1729 she had gone into full production and sold her powder throughout the country, delivering it herself to shops, markets, and roadside stands. Mrs. Clements became a wealthy woman in the process, and Durham continued to be a mustard center until the end of the nineteenth century.

There were many other manufacturers who also benefited from the popularity of mustard. One of them was Keen's from Garlic Hill in London, established in 1742 and believed to be the reason for the saying "as keen as mustard." By 1862, Keen's had merged with Messrs. Robinson and Bellville, who processed barley, and the new company held Royal warrants to supply King William IV, Queen Victoria, and Emperor Napoleon III with their products. Keen's were conscious of the need for good advertising and used memorable images and wording such as "Never eat the national dish without the national condiment." The accompanying picture showed a monarch about to knight a large piece of beef, with a page boy beside him holding the mustard. As Henry VII

⟩⟩⟩⟩⟩⟩⟩⟩ ⟨⟨⟨⟨⟨⟨⟨⟨

Grey Poupon mustard is one of the most famous in France, and the company jealously guards its reputation by keeping its mustard recipe locked in a safe. Maurice Grey revolutionized the industry in the nineteenth century by introducing new equipment which greatly speeded up production.

had inaugurated the idea of Sir Loin, it was hardly a new idea, but it sold plenty of mustard. Roast beef and mustard were by now seen as inseparable by the British public.

Colman's is another famous mustard name which remains well-known to this day. Established in Norwich, the company eventually took over Keen's in 1903. It adopted the bull's-head logo in 1850 and was granted a Royal warrant by Queen Victoria in 1866. The distinctive yellow packaging for the most famous product, mustard powder, is so well-known in Britain that Colman's simply *is* mustard to most people.

21

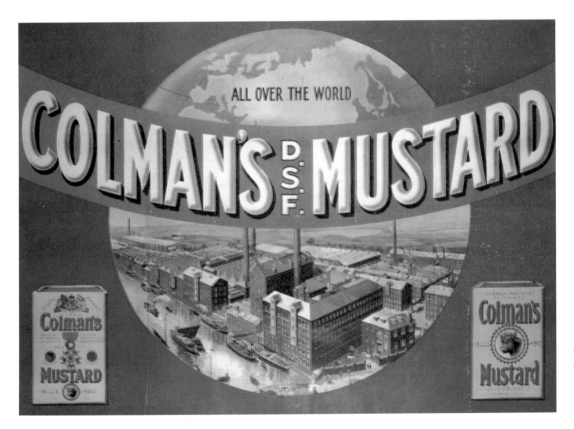

Colman's and mustard became synonymous in Britain at the beginning of this century. The company's best-known product has always been powdered mustard, but nowadays there are ready-mixed versions alongside the yellow tins of powder.

Healing Mustard

Most of us think of mustard as an essential requirement in any well-stocked modern kitchen, but we tend to forget its long and illustrious medicinal history.

It has been used for centuries as a medicinal ingredient in many different folk remedies. The important part of the plant has always been the seed, although mustard "greens," or leaves, have also been eaten for their health-giving benefits.

If mustard really did possess all the medicinal properties attributed to it, then a daily dose of it would surely help to make the world a much healthier place. Current medical opinion, however, does not rate mustard on the same level as those wonder foods, olive oil and garlic, but perhaps one day mustard will join their ranks.

The seeds contain a powerful, caustic oil, which has various properties. In the past, it was taken internally to stimulate the heart, respiratory system, and digestion. For external use, mustard powder was a common addition to hot baths, poultices, and skin plasters, used to relieve the symptoms of arthritis and rheumatism. It was also believed to help people who were suffering from colds or flu, or who were chilled by bad weather. A mustard footbath after a long, nighttime ride on horseback was a favorite restorative for tired and shivering travelers. In medieval times, huge doses of mustard were taken after excessively large or spicy meals, and in these enormous quantities it would act as an emetic and diuretic. In smaller portions, mustard would work as a stabilizer and digestive for the overburdened stomach. We still tend to eat mustard with rich and fatty foods today, as an aid to digestion. The little couplet "Sympathy without relief is like to mustard without beef" is, ironically, quite apt in this context.

The marvelous cure-all

The ancient Greeks were enthusiastic about the medicinal properties of mustard, believing that the very pungent black seeds, which are particularly sulfurous, were more health-giving than the brown or white ones. The

Hippocrates, the early Greek physician and philosopher, was an avid exponent of preventative medicine, though his views on treating illness were somewhat radical. "What cannot be cured by medicine must be cured by the knife; what cannot be cured by the knife must be cured by fire," he wrote. Mustard, especially in poultices, was an important part of his treatment to cure bronchitis, pneumonia, and rheumatism.

Aesculapius, son of Apollo, was credited with creating mustard, but its stimulating effect on the brain was in fact recognised before the time of the Greeks.

Greeks also ate the green leaves of the mustard plant, both raw and cooked, and Athenaeus mentions mustard alongside lettuce in his writings on salads. What we know today as mustard and cress is in fact unlikely to be mustard seedlings, but rather the seeds of the rape plant, though true mustard and cress was once grown from the seeds of white mustard and land cress. Athenaeus also writes about a special kind of mustard called Cyprus mustard (*napa kuprion*) which may be similar to the varieties in common use today. We do know that the Greeks cultivated mustard as a crop, rather than simply gathering it from the wild. In fact, mustard was such an important herb to the ancient Greeks that their god of medicine and healing, Aesculapius, was credited with its creation.

"Mustard burns like fire," wrote the Roman Pliny in the 1st century A.D. But he perceived it as a healing fire, citing mustard as a remedy for many ailments. He claimed that it was enough simply to place some mustard on a bite from even "the most venomous" snake to effect a cure and that eating the worst poisonous fungi was no problem if the mustard was consumed immediately afterward. Pliny wrote several volumes of his *Natural History* on the medicinal qualities of plants – based, presumably, on his own observations, though we do not know how far his practical experimentation took him. He died neither from snake bites nor lethal mushrooms, but was a victim of the great eruption that obliterated Pompeii.

Both the Greeks and the Romans considered mustard to be an excellent stimulant, rousing not only the appetite, but also the brain. They used the seeds both as an indigestion

The English name for a mustard plaster was a sinapism and in French it was sinapisme. Both words come from the Greek for white mustard Sinapsis alba. *These packs contained mustard papers which would have had a similar effect to plasters.*

treatment and as a laxative (in the latter case, white mustard seeds were thought to be particularly effective). Chewing whole seeds with food was commonly practiced as a means of flavoring meat, and also in cases of bad toothache, when the mustard oil would desensitize the inflamed gums. Other medical solutions stemmed from combining mustard seed with various liquids. One popular potion was made by infusing the seeds in heated wine or hot water. This was used as a gargle against sore throats, for treating bronchitis and congestion of the nose and chest, and even for the less threatening condition of hiccoughs.

THE MUSTARD POULTICE

One of the most traditional uses of mustard favored by the Greeks and Romans was in the form of a poultice. This hot paste could be made from all manner of ingredients, mashed or ground up with a liquid of some kind to bind everything together. Designed to draw out heat and impurities from the body and to bring the blood to the surface of the skin, poultices have been used for many different ailments throughout the ages. Some were used specifically for wounds or skin infections, others for muscular aches and pains, or to relieve internal problems such as congestion in the lungs. A mustard poultice from Greek or Roman times might have been made from ground seeds mixed with hot water, spread onto gauze, and wrapped like a

A selection of Colman's mustards for many different uses – from mustard to eat, and taken on an Arctic expedition, to bran for making poultices. Mustard was used by poultry keepers to stop hens from eating their own eggs which can commonly happen. A little mustard put onto an eggshell soon puts them off the idea.

bandage around the affected part of the body. An alternative version was a paste made from ground seeds and vinegar, applied to the body and held in place. Both were likely to cause irritation to all but the toughest skin.

Hippocrates was a great advocate of the mustard poultice, generally preferring the vinegar paste recipe, which he used to treat bronchitis, rheumatism, pneumonia, and neuralgia. Hippocrates was born into a medical family on the Greek island of Kos in the fifth century. He prescribed natural treatments, taken in conjunction with "preventative medicine," meaning a healthy diet and plenty of exercise. Though much of his time was taken up with medical matters, he also wrote several philosophical treatises, which were widely read.

The use of mustard to combat congestion and general respiratory problems was constantly being restated, especially during the Middle Ages, and its properties for aiding digestion were never disputed. John Gerard's *Herbal*, published in 1597, contains this example: "The seede of mustarde pounded with vinegar is an excellent sauce, good to be eaten with any grosse meates, either fish or flesh, because it doth help digestion, warmeth the stomach and provoketh appetitie." But according to John Evelyn, writing in 1699, mustard leaves were "of incomparable effect to quicken and revive the spirits, strengthening the memory, expelling heaviness" and therefore provoking a rather different kind of appetite for life, relieving melancholia and depression.

CULPEPER'S LORE

The poultice was still a popular remedy for all types of illness in the 17th century, when the British herbalist and physician Nicholas Culpeper recommended putting a mustard poultice (made from ground mustard seed, bread crumbs, and vinegar) on the soles of the feet as an effective way of relieving fevers, sciatica, and rheumatic pains. Vinegar was seen as another great cure-all, widely used as a medicine both internally and externally. The nursery rhyme "Jack and Jill" reminds us of its use as a dressing for bruises and wounds, wrapping poor unfortunate Jack's head "with vinegar and brown paper." Culpeper was an influential voice and remained so for many years. He first published his book *The English*

Nicholas Culpeper (1616–1654) was the most famous of the seventeenth century herbalists and physicians. He wrote the "English Physician" known today simply as Culpeper's Herbal. *Culpeper recommended the use of mustard in poultices for fevers, sciatica, and rheumatic pains.*

24

Bruise Reliever

The ingredients might suggest this is an interesting sauce, but in fact mustard seeds, onion, and honey make an effective bruise and swelling reliever.

*2 parts mustard seed,
ground with a pestle and mortar
1 part set honey
1 part finely chopped onion
Combine ingredients and apply to infected area, covering with a bandage or handkerchief.*

Gargle

A mustard gargle prepared with natural ingredients is an excellent way to fight off a sore throat.

*1 tbsp mustard seed,
ground with a pestle and mortar
juice of half a lemon
1 tbsp salt
1 tbsp clear honey
1¼ cups boiling water
Combine ingredients and leave for about 15 minutes, covered.*

>>>>>>>> <<<<<<<<

The frontispiece to The Herball *by John Gerarde published in 1597. He advocated the use of mustard as an aid to digestion and appetite.*

25

Physician Enlarged in 1653, and it was still being sold at the beginning of the nineteenth century. He advised that taking mustard was a sensible measure "whenever a stimulating medicine is wanted to act upon the nerves." By the eighteenth century, a physician named Herberden was suggesting that mustard could help in asthma attacks, presumably because of the age-old belief that it was useful for respiratory diseases and ailments.

When mustard is made into a condiment, it should never be mixed with hot water, but medicinally it has long been used in hot baths. Ground black seeds were preferred for this purpose, and though ordinary kitchen mustard powder would have been perfectly adequate for bathroom use, nineteenth century manufacturers were quick to realize the potential of such a product. They were soon packaging bath mustard in special boxes, for humans and even for horses! It was sold as a marvelous pick-me-up and soother for rheumatic pain, stiff muscles, headaches, and tired feet. Before clever packaging and marketing made mustard baths something special, ordinary people had quietly been using them for years. They were most commonly used to prevent colds and flu in the days when people were convinced that colds could be caught by getting cold or wet. The great advantage of mustard over any other remedy was that it was always very cheap to buy and easy to obtain – most houses would have kept a large pot of it in the pantry at all times.

Colman's managed to inject some style into the somewhat unappealing and messy idea of a mustard bath with its advertising campaign to promote the benefits of a long, hot soak. Just before World War I, the firm was using an illustration of elegant figures waltzing around a ballroom, under the title "After the Dance – a Mustard Bath," suggesting that it would revive anyone who had danced the night away. Two or three tablespoons of the magic powder were claimed to be enough in a good deep hot bath. Presumably it did not stain the body yellow, but nevertheless it must have been quite a task for the poor person dealing with the endless cans of hot water to fill and empty the bath, in the days when indoor plumbing and drainage were not commonplace. Another of mustard's uses was to clear a

muddy complexion by holding the head over a steaming bowl of mustard and boiling water, to open the skin's pores and remove blemishes. Mustard oil, however, was used in slightly different ways. Too powerful and irritating in its raw state, the oil had to be diluted in a carrier such as alcohol or camphor, when it could be used to treat chilblains, muscular pain, or rheumatism. Mustard oil was even used as an alternative to wearing a wig or toupee – in theory, at least, the pungent oil can be rubbed into a bald or thinning scalp to stimulate the growth of hair.

>>> <<<

Mustard Bath

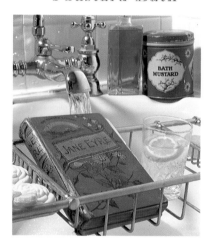

A good book, a gin and tonic, and a long hot mustard bath provide perfect relaxation.

4 tbsp mustard seeds, ground with a pestle and mortar a generous handful of bath sea salt Sprinkle the mustard and the salt together into the bathtub as it fills.

Colman's produced a special mustard for baths, packaging it in an entirely different colour and style of box to make it seem as different as possible from the for eating variety.

The footbath was the thing for anyone weary, cold, or chilled from traveling and being outdoors in wintry weather. The clever use of color in this advertisement says Colman's mustard.

COLMAN'S MUSTARD

"Returned from Klondyke"

A MUSTARD ATLAS

Armchair travelers and cooks at home can choose from a worldwide variety of different mustards. There are styles to suit every taste from Europe, America, and Asia.

FRANCE

Mustard production is still centered around Dijon, but from this one area come many different varieties.

Dijon mustard: yellow, smooth, and with a pronounced, pungent taste, made with finely ground black and brown seeds blended with liquid such as wine, verjuice (the juice from unripe grapes) or vinegar, plus spices and salt. Although it has been given an AOC (*Appelation Controlée*), with strict rules laid down about its ingredients, it can be made outside Dijon. Most French mustard, however, is still made in this region.

Bordeaux mustard: a mild flavor, using black and brown seeds, either ground fine or with some husk remaining. A darker color than Dijon, and with a subtle sweet-sourness, it includes grape must (unfermented wine), vinegar, and herbs such as tarragon.

Meaux mustard: medium hot and grainy, using partly crushed and partly ground black and brown seeds, blended with vinegar and spices. Made originally by the monks of Meaux in the early seventeenth century, the formula was given to the Pommery family in 1760. In 1826, Brilat-Savarin opined that: "the *only* mustard is Meaux mustard."

Florida mustard: mild, smooth, and pale, made with champagne (or to be strictly technical, wines that are a by-product of champagne production and which do not qualify for the champagne name). When a champagne mustard was created in 1803, the maker Bourdin said that it "has a flavor, a bouquet, an aroma easier to rejoice at than describe."

Beaujolais mustard: has a claret color and includes red ground seeds.

Champsac mustard: fragrant, smooth, dark, flavored with fennel.

Moutarde a l'ancienne: mild flavor, coarsely ground seeds.

BRITAIN

Traditionally renowned for its vivid yellow mustard powder. British mustard is composed of finely ground black, brown, and white seeds with the husks removed, wheat flour, and sugar, plus spices such as turmeric for color. Powdered mustard is made up with cold water to a paste and allowed to stand for ten minutes or so while the flavor and heat develop. Alternatively, a milk and cream combination, vinegar, or beer can be used instead of water. Various prepared mustards are also produced, including local specialty ingredients such as ale, Scotch whiskey, cider, and English wine. One company has experimented with reviving the old tradition of flavoring horseradish sauce with mustard.

ITALY

Mostarda di frutta: fruit preserved in a mustard-flavored syrup is "the" style of mustard in Italy. Commercial production is largely focused on *mostarda di Cremona*, while the other varieties are generally prepared domestically.

Mostarda di Cremona: uses whole fruit such as

Fennel

Tarragon vinegar

Cinnamon

>>>>>>>> <<<<<<<<

Peach

pears, cherries, apricots, peaches or figs, together with sliced fruits such as lemon, preserved in a syrup flavored with mustard, white wine, and honey.

Mostarda di Veneto: two versions are prepared, using either quinces or apples.

Mostarda alla Toscana (also known as *mostarda di Capri*): combines pears and apples simmered in vin santo, spiced with cinnamon, cloves, and lemon zest, preserved in a syrup of grape must, infused with mustard seeds.

Mostardo di Piedmont: pumpkins, quinces, walnuts, toasted filberts, pears, and figs, preserved in a mustard syrup based on must from Barbera grapes.

Mostarda di frutta piccante: the hottest variety, using various puréed fruits.

GERMANY

Dusseldorf mustard: usually mild, even slightly sweet and sour, though it can veer toward the full-bodied and pungent. Black mustard seeds are blended with vinegar, herbs,ßø and spices. Mid, to dark brown color.

Bavarian mustard: mild, coarse-grained.

Tafelsenf ("table· mustard"): a mild, all-purpose style.

SWEDEN

Mild, sweet mustards prepared using vinegar, sugar, and spices.

Sugar cane

UNITED STATE

American mustard: very mild, yellow paste made from white mustard seeds, vinegar or white wine, plus added spices such as turmeric and paprika.

American brown mustard: pale brown color, with a subtle spiciness.

Creole mustard: brown color, coarsely ground and sometimes mildly pungent.

Russian mustard: very hot and sweet.

CHINA

Usually made from powdered brown mustard seeds by blending with water, rice vinegar, or beer, to produce a very hot style.

Tumeric and paprika

Rice

JAPAN

Japanese mustard has neither the fragrance nor the subtlety of Western mustards. Available as a prepared paste or in powdered form, the latter is considered the superior version. Powder is made up with a little water in the base of a bowl, which is then inverted while the flavor develops, over about 15 minutes. It should be prepared just before serving, as the pungency soon fades. At its peak, though, this is strong stuff and little is needed.

29

FIRST CHOOSE YOUR FLAVOR

THE WIDE CHOICE OF FLAVORED MUSTARDS NOW AVAILABLE SUITS AN EVER-WIDER RANGE OF USES, AND, RATHER THAN CHOOSING A FLAVORED MUSTARD ACCORDING TO THE DISH YOU ARE SERVING, WHY NOT REVERSE THE ORDER, PUTTING MUSTARD FIRST, AND USING ITS FLAVOR AS A STARTING POINT FROM WHICH TO CHOOSE THE ACCOMPANYING FOOD? HERE ARE SOME FLAVORED MUSTARDS, TOGETHER WITH THEIR SUGGESTED USES.

Mustard should be stored in a cool place, and once opened the container should be kept covered (to help prevent it from drying out) and refrigerated. No matter how old mustard grows, it will not develop bacteria or mold, though the flavor will fade.

ANISEED MUSTARD
Fish, dressings (ideal for carrot, beets, tomato or cucumber salad).

REAL ALE MUSTARD
Stews, steaks, ham, sausages, robust cheeses, jacket potatoes.

BASIL MUSTARD
White meat, on pizza, quiche or tart (beneath the topping), tomatoes.

Basil

CHILI MUSTARD
Spicy soups, stews, chili con carne, sausages.

CHIVE MUSTARD
Salad dressings, in meat and fish sauces, potatoes.

CIDER VINEGAR MUSTARD
Roast pork, pork pies, ham, sausages, cheddar cheese.

COGNAC MUSTARD
White meat, stews, salad dressings.

CILANTRO MUSTARD
Spicy soups, white meats (particularly pork), rice salads.

Chilies

Horseradish

DILL MUSTARD
Cured or smoked fish (gravadlax, of course), seafoods, salad dressings, potatoes.

GARLIC MUSTARD
Various meats (especially steak, barbecued sausages, poultry stuffings), Scotch eggs, vinaigrette, mayonnaise, vegetable purées.

GINGER MUSTARD
Herrings, chicken, turkey, veal, pork, oriental dishes, sauces, dressings.

SPICED HONEY MUSTARD
Game, sweet-cured ham, smoked meats, cheese.

Ginger

HORSERADISH MUSTARD
Roast beef, cold and boiled beef, fish sauces, baked potato dishes, beet salad.

Lemons

LEMON MUSTARD
Roast chicken, veal, salad dressings, fish sauces, sautéed zucchini.

MINT MUSTARD
Lamb, especially leg, meatballs, salads, potato dishes, applesauce.

BLACK OLIVE MUSTARD
Barbecued meat, pissaladiere, dressings (ideal for tomatoes).

ORANGE MUSTARD
Cold meat such as chicken, pork and duck, salad dressings.

Peanuts

PEANUT MUSTARD
Oriental dishes, chicken, salad dressings, sandwiches.

GREEN PEPPERCORN MUSTARD
Various meats (especially steak), meat fondues, vinaigrette, deglazing, sautéed mushrooms, pancake batter.

PINK PEPPERCORN MUSTARD
Various meat, especially broiled, vegetable soups.

HERBS OF PROVENCE MUSTARD
Various meat, especially broiled, vegetable soups.

ROQUEFORT CHEESE MUSTARD
White meat (especially roast chicken), salad dressings.

SCOTCH WHISKEY MUSTARD
Cold meat, game dishes, full-flavored cheeses, meat sauces.

TARRAGON MUSTARD
White meat (ideal for roast chicken and chicken salad), dressings (especially tomato salad), soups.

VIOLET MUSTARD
Salad dressings, sauces, deli meats.

Tarragon

Violets

31

Mustard around the World

Mustard has long been a worldwide ingredient, and many countries have their own indigenous varieties, leading to a repertoire of mustard cuisine.

A selection of British Victorian main course dishes, such as sirloin of beef and leg of mutton, which without doubt would have been served with mustard for anyone who wished it.

Some of these dishes have stood the test of time, while others are currently out of fashion, but as mustard has been around for so long, some dishes which are all but forgotten now may well be rediscovered in the future. The cuisines of India, Asia, the Mediterranean, the Balkan states, the Caribbean, the U.S., northern Europe, and Africa all make use of mustard in some form or other.

France, often thought of as the true home of mustard (it still produces over half the world's output of made mustard), has a large repertoire of ways to use it, spanning classic sauces and dressings such as mayonnaise, vinaigrette, and the garlicky *aoli* to *ragouts* and *daubes*. French dressing is generally made with Dijon mustard, but a dash of the champagne-flavored version makes a special alternative. It is also good in sauces and for fish or chicken, and most spicy dishes. Sauces for vegetables and broiled meats are superbly partnered by Meaux or white wine mustard.

Among France's signature dishes are *lapin à la moutarde* (rabbit baked with mustard and served with a mustard sauce) and a variation on this theme of *poulet moutarde Dijonnaise*

Cured salmon is a Swedish specialty, invariably served with a mustard sauce.

(chicken with a wine, cream, cheese, and mustard sauce finished with bread crumbs).

Perfect partners

Northern Europe has its vast array of smoked, cured, pickled, and salted meats, which are often served with mustard of some kind. Germany has sausage specialties – probably up to 1,000 different kinds – which are tailor-made to eat with German mustard made by the country's *Senf Meisters* (master mustard makers). In the north and west of Germany, the preference is for a sharper flavor, such as that made in Dusseldorf, which perfectly complements the taste of rich dishes such as pork knuckle or full-flavored sausages. In the south, particularly in Bavaria, a mild, sweet mustard is more popular and is often eaten with *wiesswurt* (veal sausage).

In Scandinavia the taste is for a mild, sweet mustard such as that used in gravadlax, the Swedish sauce traditionally eaten with cured salmon. This sauce is flavored strongly with dill. In Denmark, a similar style of sauce accompanies roast goose.

The British love mustard with meats and fish of all kinds and frequently offer it with roast or broiled beef, hot or cold ham, pork pies and sausages. It is traditionally served with oily fish such as herrings and mackerel, and it also partners hard cheese, such as Cheddar, in sandwiches or toasted into a Welsh rarebit. This rich dish of Cheddar cheese melted with ale, mustard, and seasonings on toasted bread needs the addition of the mustard to give it "bite" and stop it from being too cloying.

British palates adore pickles and chutneys. Mustard seed has always been a classic constituent of pickling spice, along with chilies, ginger, and allspice to flavor the vinegar prior to pickling fruit or vegetables.

In Italy mustard takes on yet another form in the shape of *mostarda di frutta* (fruit flavored with a syrup containing mustard oil or seed), with many different regional variations. There is *mostarda di Cremona*, including pears, apricots, cherries, plums, peaches, melons, and figs, or *mostarda alla Toscana*, with apples and

>>>>>>><<<<<<<

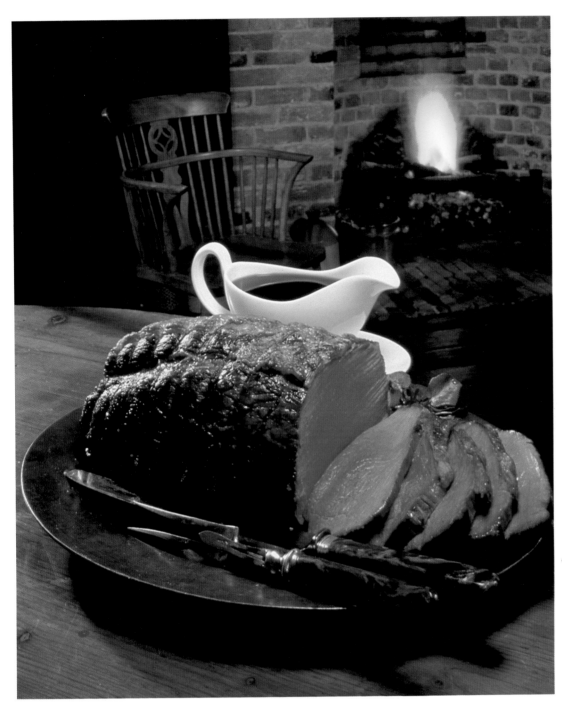

Roast beef, traditionally served with mustard, is the national dish in Britain: it has earned the British the nickname "rostbifs" in France.

33

A wonderfully elaborate and beautifully decorated jar designed to hold the Italian specialty Mostarda di Frutta. Different regions of the country have their own specialties.

pears cooked in *vin santo*. This often accompanies *bollito misto*, the classic dish of boiled meats, or *zampona di Modena* (a boned pig's trotter stuffed with pork, bacon, and truffles), ham, eels, and cotechino (a spicy pork sausage) served with lentils. In Lombardy, where pasta vies with rice and polenta as a staple food, *mostarda di Cremona* is mixed with pumpkin to stuff a *tortelli di zucca*.

Yet another "mostarda" comes from the Veneto region and is eaten with goose, baked ham or pork, while in Piedmont a local version of fruits and nuts in a syrup made from must from the Barbera grape accompanies Taleggio cheese or boiled meats. There is one very hot version, good with boiled meats, known as *mostarda di frutta piccante* and based on puréed fruits. Its origins are probably very old, from the days when sweet and sour flavors were used more often than now, but all these mostardas are certainly an original taste in these days of international cuisine.

Although Americans enjoy a wide variety of mustards, when it comes to hot dogs it must be the smooth, sweet "ball-park" type.

34

MUSTARD ON THE MOVE

Americans love to eat on the move and mustard goes with them, chiefly in hot dogs and hamburgers, but also in deli-style sandwiches such as pastrami on rye. The American style of mustard tends to be smooth, mild, and quite sweet, with a texture that makes it easy to squirt along a frankfurter single-handed. But it does not appear only at the ball-park and is equally effective in more traditional cooking.

Mustard was first brought to America with the early settlers, and soon trails of golden flowers marked the places where the first settlers had traveled. By the beginning of the twentieth century, mustard was commonplace in the U. S., but not particularly popular, so Francis French, a New York State mustard manufacturer, set his plant superintendent the task of producing a really successful formula.

This he did, creating a mild, creamy mustard which by 1915 had made sales of a million dollars for the company. In 1926 French's sold out to Colman's, and nowadays in the U.S. there are over 50 brands of specialty mustard, from Russian-style to extra hot Chinese, to suit every palate and every style of food.

A more traditional use of mustard can be found in the southern states, where Virginia hams are still stuffed with a combination of sweet peppers and various greens, such as cabbage and spinach, before being spiked with mustard seed and Tabasco sauce. Mustard seeds blend into Cajun seasoning along with stalwarts such as pepper, cayenne, and garlic. In this region mustard greens are often cooked as a vegetable.

THE ORIENTAL APPROACH

A major characteristic of Indian cuisine involves the blending of different spices together, and mustard seed frequently appears in various styles of seasoning. This does not, however, add the pungency that might be expected – the seeds are heated, giving them a nutty quality, and once ground, a slight bitterness develops which is considered a digestive aid. In the south of India, spice blends tend to be hotter than their northern counterparts, combining mustard seeds with hot favorites such as chilies, curry leaves, cilantro, turmeric, and ginger. Mustard seeds are also used whole to season various foods such as vegetables and legumes, and for preparing relishes and chutneys, which are served with Indian breads or to accompany main courses. Mustard seed oil is used, particularly in Bengal and Kashmir, as a cooking medium. Its pungency when raw is transformed through heating into a sweet, nutty flavor. Cooked mustard leaves are also served.

Sri Lanka mustard seed is usually fried in oil, before being finely ground and blended with other spices to make curry powder. The seeds can also be used coarsely ground and sprinkled over food as an individual seasoning. Mustard paste, which is a combination of black and brown seeds with other ingredients such as vinegar, garlic, ginger, and sugar, is served with stews and curries.

The Chinese mix water or vinegar with a powerful mustard powder to make a pungent sauce, served with deep-fried food such as egg rolls. They also combine it with other flavorings such as sesame oil, vinegar, and chili to make

The tradition of pickling fresh vegetables in order to preserve them is widespread throughout the world, and mustard seeds are a favourite flavoring for the preserving liquid.

dipping sauces. The mustard plant is also widely used, with numerous different leafy varieties which are also used for their roots – these are sometimes pickled and used in meat dishes.

Japanese mustard, *karashi*, is one of the principal flavorings placed on the dining table, alongside soy sauce, rice vinegar, pepper, and wasabi (Japanese horseradish). *Karashi* is traditionally served with a slow-fried dish of pork cutlet coated in bread crumbs and accompanied by cabbage. Japanese noodles are the fast food of the cuisine, and versions such as *Hiyashi-chuka* (cold ramen noodles with ham, vegetables, omelet and beansprouts) are served in a soy, sesame, and vinegar sauce. The pickles eaten after a main course are often prepared using mustard and wasabi.

Chinese mustard is always freshly made before serving, and so retains its fiery flavour to add piquancy to egg rolls and other dim sum dishes.

Curry spice mixtures usually include mustard seeds, and mustard oil is popular for frying.

FROM THE SEED TO THE POT

THE WAY MUSTARD IS MADE TODAY SCARCELY VARIES FROM METHODS WE KNOW OUR ANCESTORS USED. MACHINES AND TECHNOLOGY MADE THE JOB EASIER AND FASTER, BUT THE FINISHED RESULTS ARE PROBABLY MUCH THE SAME NOW AS THEY HAVE ALWAYS BEEN.

The manufacture of mustard is highly sophisticated, as all food processing is today, but it has kept very much to its roots, with little change to the ingredients or the way they are manipulated into powdered or ready-made mustards. We may have a huge variety of specialty mustards to choose from, but the basic recipes are still adhered to, and mustard is one of the few food stuffs which seems to have kept its quality and remained unadulterated. Strict codes and controls, particularly in France, have probably been partly responsible for this high standard, but it is interesting that we expect our mustard to taste as it always has and not to be adapted or updated.

Although mustard seed is grown on a huge scale worldwide and the industry is vast, the processes of harvesting, threshing, grinding, and blending, while mechanized, are still the same as they always have been, and the mustard in the pot tastes as delicious as ever.

The ground seed is ready to be mixed with liquids or dry ingredients and blended into different types of mustard.

6

The mustard seeds must be harvested at exactly the right stage of ripeness and before the seeds begin to fall.

1

For some mustards which require a smoother texture, the husks around the seed are removed.

5

2

The seeds must be dried, either in old-fashioned stooks or in modern kilns, to the right degree of moisture.

Depending on how they will be used, the seeds are ground to flour or just lightly crushed.

4

3

The tiny seeds are threshed from the small, dry, pea-like pods and are checked for quality before being sifted to remove debris.

It is often easy to f... that a delicio... sophisticated mustard ... it all to a humble w... brown, or black ...

CHAPTER ONE

APPETIZERS

Any first course should be piquant and delicious, light and stimulating. Mustard has all the right qualities to add just what is needed to such dishes. Popular with cheese and eggs, subtle in soups, and powerful with more robust flavors, it starts any meal off with great style.

APPETIZERS

Mustard is the perfect instant flavoring for many quick and simple appetizers. It can be added straight from the jar to dressings, sauces, soups, and all manner of fresh light dishes to start a meal or to make a snack. Crudités with a dip or sauce are perennially popular. Provide mild whole-grain mustards or mayonnaise flavored with mustard as a dip, and a selection of the freshest raw vegetables arranged on a serving dish. Salad dressings are transformed by the imaginative use of seasonings, particularly by the careful addition of mustard. Give a new twist to grated carrot in a lemony dressing by finishing it with a sprinkling of black mustard seeds heated in a little oil until they pop, to make a refreshing salad with an Indian savor. Fish and seafood have long been favorite appetizers. Gravadlax or marinated salmon has become a fashionable alternative to smoked salmon; a mustard and dill sauce, slightly sweet and quite thick, marries beautifully with the fish.

Two men and a woman pouring wine, *Velasquez, 1618*

CELERIAC SOUP *with* THYME-INFUSED PISTACHIOS

Hearty enough for a family supper, this easy-to-make soup is sufficiently sophisticated in flavor to offer to dinner party guests. The thyme-infused pistachios sprinkled on top add a distinctive quality which can be used to elevate many other soups. Stirred in at the last moment, the mustard imparts quite a strong flavor; add just one tablespoon and taste before adding a second.

SERVES 4

1 celeriac (about 1lb)
¼ cup butter
1 onion, chopped
1 leek, sliced
3 cups vegetable or chicken broth
2tsp vegetable oil

2tbsp shelled pistachio nuts, roughly chopped
1 sprig thyme, roughly chopped
⅞ cup milk
salt and freshly ground black pepper
5tbsp heavy cream
1-2tbsp wholegrain mustard

Heat the oven to 375°F.

Roughly chop the celeriac, placing the pieces in water to prevent discoloration.

Melt the butter in a large saucepan over a medium heat, add the onion and leek and sauté for about 2 minutes until soft. Add the chopped celeriac and sauté for a further minute. Pour in the broth, bring to a boil and simmer for 10 minutes, or until the celeriac is tender.

Meanwhile, to infuse the chopped pistachio nuts with the thyme, pour the oil into a small roasting pan and heat over a high heat. Put the pistachio nuts and the thyme into the pan and roast in the oven for about 4 minutes.

Remove the cooked vegetables from the heat and allow to cool slightly. Purée them in a food processor and return to a clean pan. Add the milk, season and heat through.

Stir the cream and mustard into the soup and gently heat through. Serve the soup sprinkled with the thyme-infused pistachio nuts.

CRUDITÉS *with* MUSTARD DIPS

A common *hors d'oeuvre* of the French countryside, crudités (raw vegetables) are an excellent and easy way to enjoy fresh, healthy fare. The selection of dips given here provides a variety of mustardy flavors to accompany the crudités. The nutty dip is inspired by a sophisticated sauce recipe devised in ancient Rome.

SERVES 4

4 carrots, peeled and cut into
    strips
4 sticks celery, cut into strips
10 scallions spring onions, each
    trimmed and cut in half
1 small cauliflower, broken
    into flowerets
1 cucumber, cut in half across
    and then into strips
8 cherry tomatoes, halved
EGGPLANT DIP
1 eggplant (about ½lb)
1 head garlic, unpeeled
1tbsp French mustard
2tbsp olive oil

salt and freshly ground black
    pepper
MUSTARD DIP
6tbsp plain yogurt
6tbsp sour cream
2tbsp wholegrain mustard
1tbsp chopped fresh tarragon,
    or 1tsp dried tarragon
NUTTY DIP
3tbsp pine nuts, finely ground
3tbsp ground almonds
1tsp English mustard
3tbsp olive oil
4tbsp fromage frais

To make the Mustard Dip and the Nutty Dip, combine the ingredients for each dip in a bowl.

To make the Eggplant Dip, heat the oven to 400°F. Prick the skin of the eggplant in several places, place it on a baking tray with the head of garlic and bake in the heated oven for 25 minutes. When the eggplant is cooked, remove the tray from the oven and allow the eggplant to cool slightly before carefully removing the skin. Squeeze the garlic purée from the cooked cloves. Place the eggplant meat in a food processor, add half of the garlic purée and the remaining ingredients, and mix well. (The unused half of the purée can be mixed into soups, sauces or used as a sandwich spread.)

To serve, transfer each dip to a small clean dish, place them in the center of a serving platter and arrange all the raw vegetables around. Alternatively, arrange a selection of vegetables on individual dishes with some of each dip on the side.

The clear, fresh flavors and crisp textures of recently harvested and prepared vegetables highlight mustard's subtleties and depths.

44

SPICY CRAB CLAWS

This is a wonderfully messy dish to serve to your guests. Provide plenty of finger bowls and paper napkins and invite your friends to tuck in. If the claws still have their shells, you will need crackers and picks for digging out the last bits of meat. The mustard adds heat, reinforcing the effect of the chili peppers.

SERVES 4

2tbsp vegetable oil
4 shallots, finely chopped
1 clove garlic, crushed
2 red chili peppers, finely chopped
1¼ cups fish or vegetable broth
7½oz can chopped tomatoes
1tsp English mustard
salt and freshly ground black pepper
16-24 crab claws, depending on size
1 loaf crusty bread, optional

Heat the oil in a large saucepan, put in the shallots, garlic and chili peppers and cook gently for about 4 minutes until soft but not brown.

Pour in the broth and add the chopped tomatoes. Stir in the mustard, season and then bring to a boil. Add the crab claws, lower the heat and simmer for 3 minutes.

Using a slotted spoon, remove the crab claws to either a large serving dish or four individual dishes. Pour the spicy sauce over the top and serve immediately. Provide plenty of crusty bread for mopping up any leftover sauce.

Mini Chicken Kabobs *cooked in a* Mustard Marinade

The unmistakable mustardy flavor of these dainty kabobs will delight all mustard lovers. Marinating the chicken in yogurt helps to tenderize it, with the result that the cooked kabobs really melt in the mouth. Soak 8-10 small wooden skewers in water for 10 minutes before using to prevent them from burning.

SERVES 4

⅔ cup plain yogurt
1 lime, juice only
salt and freshly ground black pepper

3 chicken breasts, skinned and boned
2tbsp coarse grain mustard
selection of salad leaves
lime wedges for garnish

In a bowl, combine 3 tablespoons of yogurt with the lime juice and season with salt and black pepper. Cut the chicken breasts into 1-inch cubes and mix into the yogurt and lime mixture. Cover and leave to marinate for 2 hours.

Meanwhile, combine the remaining yogurt with the mustard and some black pepper to make a basting mixture. Heat the broiler to medium.

Remove the chicken from the marinade and thread the pieces onto small skewers. Grill the kabobs on one side for 5 minutes. Turn, baste generously with the mustard mixture and broil for a further 5 minutes. Increase the heat to high, turn the kabobs once more, baste again and broil for 5 minutes more, or until the chicken is cooked.

Serve with a selection of salad leaves and garnish with lime wedges.

Three-Cheese Tarts

These tarts are ideal appetizers and can be served at buffets or taken on a picnic. The mustard flavor is intense, but you can reduce the amount if you prefer.

SERVES 4

Pastry
⅔ cup flour
pinch salt
3tbsp firm margarine or butter, diced
Filling
2tbsp butter
1 red onion, thinly sliced
1 egg, beaten
½ cup milk
1tbsp honey

2tbsp coarse grain mustard
¼ cup crumbled Dolcelatte cheese
¼ cup freshly grated Parmesan cheese
¼ cup chopped Bel Paese cheese
salt and freshly ground black pepper
selection of lettuce leaves

First make the pastry. Sift the flour into a bowl with the salt. Add the diced margarine or butter and cut through the flour with a knife. When each piece of butter is coated with flour, rub it into the flour with your fingertips only until the mixture resembles fine bread crumbs. Add 1½ tablespoons of water and bring the mixture together to form a ball of dough. Chill in the refrigerator, covered, for at least 30 minutes.

Remove the chilled pastry from the refrigerator, allow it to stand 10 minutes then roll it out to about ¼ inch thick. Cut out pastry circles large enough to line four 4-inch diameter tart pans. Line the pans with the pastry and prick the base of each circle a few times with a fork. Chill the lined pans for 30 minutes; this allows the pastry to relax and prevents shrinkage during cooking.

Meanwhile, make the filling. Melt the butter in a saucepan and add the sliced onion. Cook over a medium-low heat for 20 minutes, stirring occasionally to make sure the onions remain evenly coated with butter.

Heat the oven to 375°F. Place a few baking beans or crumpled foil in the base of each tartcrust and bake them blind for 6 minutes.

Combine all the remaining filling ingredients except for the lettuce with the caramelized onions. Push down any tartcrust base that has risen with the back of a spoon. Fill each tartcrust to just below the rim with the filling and bake for 20-25 minutes until the tops are golden brown and the filling has set.

Serve each tart on a bed of salad leaves.

46

Welsh Rarebit Soufflé

This inspired soufflé incorporates the essential elements of a traditional Welsh Rarebit – cheese, ale and mustard. Ask your guests to take their places before taking the soufflé out of the oven as it will sink very quickly once removed. You can use this recipe to make either one large soufflé or four individual ones.

SERVES 4

2tbsp butter, plus extra for greasing
¼ cup fresh bread crumbs
¼ cup plain flour
4tbsp milk

3tbsp beer or ale
½ cup grated mature Cheddar cheese
3 eggs, separated
2tbsp English mustard

Heat the oven to 375°F. Grease the soufflé dish or four individual casserole dishes with butter and sprinkle the bottom and sides with the bread crumbs.

Melt the butter in a saucepan, add the flour and mix well. Pour in the milk gradually, stirring to prevent any lumps from forming. Stir in the beer and grated cheese. Remove from the heat and add the egg yolks and the mustard.

Beat the egg whites until they form soft peaks. A good test to make sure they are sufficiently beaten is to hold the beaters upright with some mixture on them; the mixture should remain firm but with the top of the peak drooping slightly.

Add one tablespoon of beaten egg white to the sauce and fold in. Gently fold in the remaining egg white.

Pour the soufflé mixture into the prepared dish or small dishes and bake in the center of the oven for 18-20 minutes for a large dish or 8-10 minutes for individual ones. The soufflé should be golden brown on top and will be slightly moist in the center.

Celtic Treat

Welsh rabbit, confusingly, contains no meat, but is simply melted cheese on hot buttered toast. (Rarebit is a fanciful coinage dating from the eighteenth century.) And mustard is a vital ingredient, not only because the flavors of cheese and mustard complement each other so well; the mustard also acts as an emulsifier, preventing the fat from separating out of cheese as it cooks, and so stabilizing the mixture.

GOUJONS *of* PLAICE *with* MUSTARD *and* HERB CRUST

The inspiration behind this dish is the herbed bread crumb coating devised by a resourceful fourteenth-century chef for an impromptu chicken supper when he and his master, France's King Charles VI, were campaigning near Sainte-Menehould. A mustard sauce accompanied that dish, but here the mustard is incorporated into the coating, which translates admirably to white fish. Lemon wedges, a crisp salad and one or two of the dipping sauces, such as those on pages 66 and 67, complement fish strips.

SERVES 4

1½lb flounder fillets
3 eggs, beaten
3tsp English mustard
1 cup fresh bread crumbs

3tbsp mixed fresh herbs, finely
   chopped (such as parsley,
   thyme, oregano)
vegetable oil for deep frying.

Wash and pat dry the flounder fillets and cut them into thin strips about 5 inches long by ½ inch thick.

Combine the beaten eggs and mustard in a bowl. In another bowl combine the bread crumbs and herbs. Dip each strip of fish into the egg mixture and then into the bread crumb mixture.

Pour oil into a frying pan until it is 3 inches deep and heat it until a cube of bread dropped in sizzles and immediately floats to the surface. Deep-fry the goujons in batches for about 2 minutes until crisp and golden, gently moving them around with a slotted spoon to ensure even cooking. Drain the goujons on paper towels, then serve.

>>>>>>> <<<<<<<

GRUYÈRE *and* HAM CROISSANTS

Coarse grain mustard makes its own strong, crunchy contribution to this light but satisfying snack, while binding together the flavors of the other ingredients. Quick and easy to prepare, the filled croissants can be served as part of a brunch, for a quick lunch, or for light supper.

SERVES 4

½ cup grated Gruyère cheese
4 slices ham, roughly chopped
1½tbsp coarse grain mustard

4 croissants
butter, optional
mixed salad leaves for garnish

Place the cheese, ham and mustard in a bowl and mix well. Slice open the croissants, warm under the broiler and spread with butter if using. Fill each croissant generously with the cheese mixture.

Serve with a generous garnish of fresh mixed salad leaves.

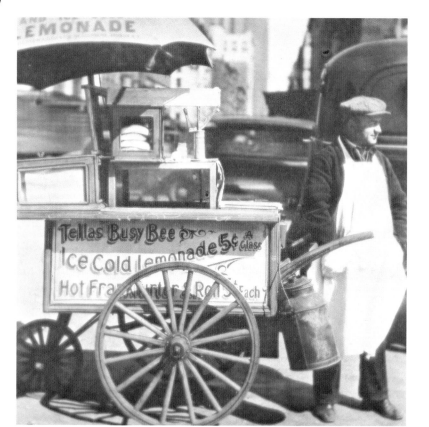

Hot Dogs

Hot Dogs are as traditionally American as apple pie. They first appeared in the 1920s, and a popular cartoon of the time featuring a dachshund helped to fix the name in the public's imagination. And no true American would eat a hot dog without a liberal helping of bright yellow, mild, slightly sweet mustard. The mustard flows over the sausage and then seeps into the bread. As the eater bites into the "dog," the mustard oozes out of the sides of the roll, leaving a yellow tide mark around the mouth. This is cleared by a well-practiced lick of the tongue.

≫≫≫≫≫≫≫≪≪≪≪≪≪≪

Salmon Gravadlax *with a* Mustard Sauce

Gravadlax (salmon cured in salt, dill and peppercorns) is an essential ingredient of the Scandinavian smorgasbord. In less grand presentations, humble bread and butter is the ideal accompaniment. The dish takes some time to cure, but it is well worth the wait.

SERVES 4

1½lb fresh salmon, middle cut, halved along the backbone, backbone and other bones removed
1 large bunch dill
1tbsp sugar
3tbsp coarse sea salt
1tbsp crushed peppercorns

Mustard sauce
2tbsp whole grain mustard
1tbsp sugar
2tbsp white wine vinegar
4tbsp olive oil
freshly chopped dill
salt and freshly ground black pepper

Scrape the scales off the salmon and pat it dry with paper towels.

Place a handful of dill on a large plate and place one half of the salmon on top, skin side down. Combine the sugar, salt and peppercorns and sprinkle over the salmon. Add another handful of dill and cover with the remaining salmon half, skin side up. Cover with the remaining dill. Cover the entire plate with plastic wrap and place a plate on top, weighted down with a heavy object. Place in the refrigerator for at least 48 hours but not more than 3 days. Baste the salmon twice each day with the juices produced, separating the salmon halves slightly to baste inside them.

To make the mustard sauce, combine the mustard, sugar and vinegar in a bowl. Gradually add the oil, beating continuously. Add the dill and salt and pepper to taste.

When ready to serve, remove the salmon from the refrigerator, scrape clean and pat dry. Slice thinly using a sharp knife and avoiding the skin; slice from left to right or right to left rather than from top to bottom.

Serve with the mustard sauce.

Mustard Pots

Because mustard has always been used as a table condiment to serve with food, as well as an ingredient in the kitchen, there have always been containers specially designed to hold it. By the eighteenth century, exquisite examples of cruet sets were being produced by master craftsmen. The three main condiments were catered for – salt, pepper, and mustard. In today's less formal world, we are likely to just put the mustard jar straight on the table, but in the more leisurely and genteel days of, say, two centuries ago, the freshly made mustard would be spooned into a little blue glass dish that stood inside a gleaming silver mustard pot.

In the Middle Ages, mustard was sold in narrow-necked jars to keep as much air as possible from reaching the mustard. Parchment was stretched over the top and tightly tied, to keep evaporation to a minimum. No doubt these jars were put straight on the table in all but the grandest households. However, domestic pots were being made even then, usually from pewter. Over the next few hundred years, other materials began to be used for pots – gold plate or silver for the rich, and glass, china or porcelain for everyone else. It is possible that mustard spoons made from animal horn first appeared around the same time. Horn mustard spoons can still be bought today. The smooth, natural material seems exactly right for the purpose, never tainting the mustard or tarnishing, as silver would.

The history and development of commercial French mustard pots is fascinating; they slowly changed shape as manufacturing methods changed and modernized, and the need for good seals was realized. Some of the oldest pots are simple and beautiful, always with a narrow neck and invariably with printed or written details of the place of origin and type of mustard. By the twentieth century, all kinds of inventive containers had been introduced as a means of boosting sales and attracting new customers. In France, mustard was often packed in small, reusable glasses which could be cleaned and used on the table for water once empty. In Britain, mustard pots have been turned into savings banks and other novelties in the past, and early mechanical cigarette lighters were made from Colman's mustard boxes.

The French mustard producer Antoine Maille offered nearly a hundred different mustards to his clients, and these pots, dated 1747, were from a period of great success for his company. The simple, peasant style of decoration was then very popular.

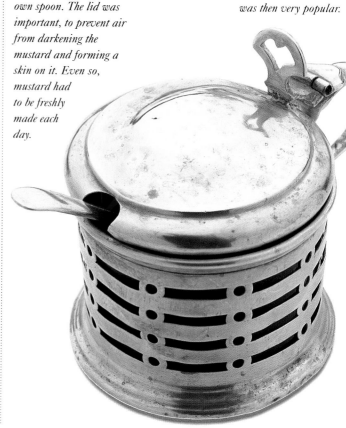

A silver mustard pot with a hinged lid and its own spoon. The lid was important, to prevent air from darkening the mustard and forming a skin on it. Even so, mustard had to be freshly made each day.

52

*T*he handles on this nineteenth-century pot are unusual, but the basic shape is the familiar one which has remained unchanged for centuries.

A fine, elegant Georgian silver mustard pot on decorative legs. No doubt it would have been part of a set, including a salt-dish in the same style, but without a lid, and a pepper grinder.

*M*ustard spoons were usually in keeping with the style of the pot. A wooden spoon was common for everyday use.

A large-scale earthenware hand-decorated French mustard jar from the 18th century. This shape, with a narrow neck and bulbous sides, was traditional and remained the same whatever the size of the pot.

53

CHAPTER TWO

Salads

Good salads need a light hand and sensitive touch to compose them and an eye for colorful but tasty combinations. The most important part though, is always the dressing. Whether this is a creamy mayonnaise or pungent vinaigrette, mustard is the key element in creating a delicious result.

SALADS

Far removed from the usual combination of lettuce, tomato, and cucumber, a salad today is likely to be the star dish of a meal with ingredients ranging from grilled vegetables, earthy legumes, fresh seafood or unusual cheeses. But, however excitingly the salad is put together, it will need a good dressing, and good dressings need mustard.

A carefully made vinaigrette with grainy mustard can turn a plateful of salad leaves into a full-scale meal. Add a sprinkling of other ingredients such as crisp bacon in little strips or melted goat's cheese, or leave the mixed leaves plain and simple. Use the best oil and wine vinegar or lemon juice you can lay your hands on and have fun choosing an appropriate mustard.

>>>>>>>><<<<<<<<

Still life with asparagus, *Louis Moillon, 1630*

>>>>>>>> <<<<<<<<

WARM ROASTED VEGETABLE SALAD

A mustard dressing seems to bring out the best in vegetables, especially when they are served warm. As well as being a substantial accompaniment to a main meal, this warm salad can be served as an appetizer. The crisp herb croutons should be added at the last moment to prevent them from soaking up too much dressing. Allow time to prepare the eggplant before you make the salad.

SERVES 4

1 eggplant
salt
6tbsp olive oil
2 red sweet peppers, seeded
    and cut into eighths
2 zucchini, cut into
    1in circles
2 small red onions, peeled
    and cut into eighths
1 small bunch thyme
freshly ground black pepper
3 cloves garlic, cut in half
1tbsp freshly chopped oregano,
    or 2tsp dried oregano

4 slices white bread, crusts
    removed and cut into
    ½in cubes
1 Italian mozzarella cheese,
    torn into small pieces
½ cup whole black olives, such
    as kalamata
DRESSING
4tbsp extra virgin olive oil
1tbsp balsamic vinegar
1tbsp lemon juice
1tsp Dijon mustard
salt and freshly ground black
    pepper

Cut the eggplant in half lengthwise and sprinkle with salt. Leave for at least 1 hour, then rinse under cold water, peel and cut into 1 inch cubes.

Heat the oven to 400°F.

Pour 4 tablespoons of the olive oil into a large roasting pan and heat over a hot burner. Add the eggplants, sweet peppers, zucchinis and onions and mix well. Add the thyme, some salt and plenty of freshly ground black pepper. Cover with foil, place in the oven and bake for about 30 minutes. Remove the pan from the oven, turn all the vegetables and return to the oven. Bake, uncovered, for a further 30 minutes until cooked.

Meanwhile, combine all the dressing ingredients in a bowl and mix well. Rub the sides of the serving dish with two of the garlic halves, then discard them.

Remove the cooked vegetables from the oven and transfer to a serving dish. Then make the croutons. Heat the remaining olive oil in a skillet over a high heat, fry the remaining garlic halves for 1 minute, then discard the garlic.

Put the cubes of bread in the pan with the chopped oregano and sauté for about 2 minutes, shaking the pan frequently, until the croutons are golden brown.

Toss the mozzarella pieces and olives through the vegetables, pour on the dressing and top with the croutons.

Temples to Mustard

The Mount Horeb Mustard Museum, in Mount Horeb, Wisconsin, houses the largest collection of mustards in the world. It was opened in 1989 by its curator, Barry Levenson, with just 365 mustards. By January 1995 the number had risen to over 2,000, including examples from such far-flung places as Guatemala and Siberia. The museum has its own wittily informative and practical newsletter, The Proper Mustard. It also sells mustards and mustard paraphenalia such as mustard cookbooks, pots, T-shirts, mugs and toy cars and even has its own university-style pennant.

Colman's Mustard Shop and Museum in Bridewell Alley, Norwich, England, is very different. Established in 1973 as part of the 150th anniversary celebrations of the founding of the firm, it concentrates on the considerable role of Colman's in the history of mustard production. It contains displays of traditional mustard production methods, and sells a selection of mustards and associated products, such as pots, aprons and so on, bearing the company name.

59

Summer Salad Bowl

A glass serving bowl is an ideal way to show off this layered salad as a centerpiece. If you want to make the salad in advance of serving, coat the avocado slices with lemon juice as you cut them to prevent discoloration.

SERVES 4

¼ red cabbage, shredded
½ iceburg lettuce, shredded or torn
1 carrot, grated
1 beefsteak tomato, sliced
1 red onion, thinly sliced
1 avocado, stone removed, peeled, and thinly sliced

DRESSING
⅝ cup plain yogurt
1tsp coarse grain mustard
4tbsp olive oil
2tbsp white wine vinegar
salt and freshly ground black pepper

Layer up a large serving bowl (with an approximate capacity of 1 gallon with the raw vegetables to make contrasting bands of color.

Combine all the dressing ingredients in a bowl and pour evenly over the top of the salad. Allow the dressing to filter through for about 10 minutes before serving.

Roast Beef Salad
with Mustard Sauce

The sauce in this recipe is quite piquant. If, when you taste it, you would prefer a milder version, add two tablespoons of sour cream and mix well.

SERVES 4

2tbsp mayonnaise
1tbsp French mustard
2tsp creamed horseradish
1tbsp lemon juice
20 stoned black olives, roughly chopped

4 scallions, thinly sliced
freshly ground black pepper
12 thin slices cooked roast beef (about ¾lb)
1 bunch watercress, washed and trimmed

With the exception of the roast beef and the watercress, combine all the ingredients together in a bowl to make the sauce.

Divide the watercress among four plates, arrange 3 slices of roast beef on top and spoon some sauce over.

Growing Your Own Mustard

To grow sweet and slightly peppery salad garnish, use white mustard seeds, brassica alba. *It is fun, and very easy, to grow them in shapes, as in the playing card symbols shown here. Simply place a template of your chosen design on damp cloth, absorbent wool or tissues, and press firmly to make an indentation. Then sprinkle a thin layer of mustard seeds in the shape. Keep them moist. After two weeks they should be about 2 inches high, when they are ready to eat.*

Fruity Duck Salad

Barbary duck, which is leaner and has a more mature flavor than other breeds, is particularly suited to the lively ingredients of this dish, but if it is unavailable any breed of duck can be used. As the mustard content is quite high, giving a strong savor, the decision as to exactly how much to include is a matter of personal taste. The dish may be served warm or cold.

SERVES 4

3 oranges, juice only	*¼ cup dried apricots*
1 lime, juice only	*1-1½ tbsp whole grain mustard,*
1 tbsp soy sauce	*according to taste*
2-3 Barbary duck breasts	*freshly ground black pepper*
(about 1¼ lb), with skin	*selection of salad leaves*

Combine the orange and lime juices with the soy sauce in a bowl. Using a sharp knife, make 3 or 4 shallow incisions across the fleshy sides of the duck breasts. Place the duck breasts in the citrus juice and soy mixture, cover with plastic wrap and leave to marinate for 4-5 hours.

Meanwhile, place the apricots in a bowl, pour in enough boiling water to cover, and leave to soak for 10 minutes. Purée the softened apricots with the soaking water either in a food processor or by passing them through a strainer. Mix in the mustard and black pepper.

Remove the duck breasts from the marinade, reserving the latter, and place under a hot broiler. Broil for 5-6 minutes on each side, basting a few times with the reserved marinade. The cooking time will vary according to the size of the duck breasts; test by cutting a small slice from the end of one breast to see if it is done to your liking. Remove from the broiler and allow to cool slightly. Remove the skin and slice each breast thinly.

Add about 6 tablespoons of the reserved marinade to the apricot sauce and mix well.

To serve, arrange the duck slices on a selection of salad leaves with a portion of apricot sauce by the side.

MIXED TOMATO SALAD *with* MUSTARD DRESSING

In summer months, many varieties of tomato become available making it possible to create a visually stimulating salad. A good mix might be one beefsteak, eight yellow, and/or red cherry tomatoes and six others, including perhaps flavia, but it does depend on what you can find. As the tomatoes in the grocery store tend not to be fully ripened, buy them a week in advance and let them finish ripening at home.

SERVES 4

1½-2lb selection of ripe
   tomatoes
6tbsp extra virgin olive oil
2tbsp balsamic vinegar
1tbsp freshly squeezed lime juice
1 clove garlic, quartered

2tsp coarse grain mustard
   tarragon
salt and freshly ground black
   pepper
2tbsp chopped fresh tarragon,
   or 2tsp dried

Cut any large tomatoes into eighths, medium-sized ones into quarters, and cherry tomatoes in half.

   Combine all the remaining ingredients except the tarragon and mix well. Pour the dressing over the tomatoes, making sure that they are completely coated. Sprinkle on the tarragon and serve.

Seeds of War

Alexander III (356–323 B.C.), also known as Alexander the Great, was one of the greatest generals in history. He laid the foundations for the Hellenistic world of territorial kingdoms, and in the process became a legendary hero. One of his greatest conquests was the defeat of the Persian empire in a series of battles. During one of them, in 335 B.C., Alexander was sent a bag of mustard seeds by Darius II, Emperor of Persia. The quantity of the seeds symbolized the enormous number of troops under his command. Alexander responded by sending back a bag of mustard seeds, to show his fiery strength of purpose.

It was in the year 1760 that a superior of the ancient religious order of Meaux transmitted to the Pommery family the secret recipe of their marvelous specialty "Moutarde des Chanoines", the Abbot's Mustard. This mustard has been served at the tables of the kings of France since 1632.

Mustard Pom
PRODUCT OF FRANCE

MOUTARDE de ME
POMMERY
AROMATISÉE AU VINA

NET WT 2

>>>>>>>><<<<<<<<

ORANGE *and* BEAN SPROUT SALAD

Roasted pumpkin seeds give this refreshing, crunchy salad a wonderful smoky flavor while the mustard in the dressing stands up manfully to the strong taste of the oranges. Crisp and colorful, it is a perfect dish for lunch in the backyard on a summer's day.

SERVES 4

1 cup fresh bean sprouts
2 cups rocket, stemmed, washed, dried and torn
1 cup selection of salad leaves, washed, dried and torn
2 oranges
2tbsp pumpkin seeds

DRESSING

1tbsp freshly squeezed orange juice
½tsp freshly grated ginger
1tbsp white wine vinegar
5tbsp olive oil
2tsp honey
1½tbsp coarse grain mustard
salt and freshly ground black pepper

Heat the oven to 400°F.

In a large bowl, mix the bean sprouts, rocket and lettuce leaves together. Remove the peel and pith from the oranges and cut into segments.

Place the pumpkin seeds on a baking sheet and roast in the oven for 5 minutes.

Mix all the dressing ingredients together, pour onto the bean sprouts and salad leaves and toss thoroughly. Scatter the orange segments on top and sprinkle the freshly roasted pumpkin seeds over them.

>>>>>>>> <<<<<<<<

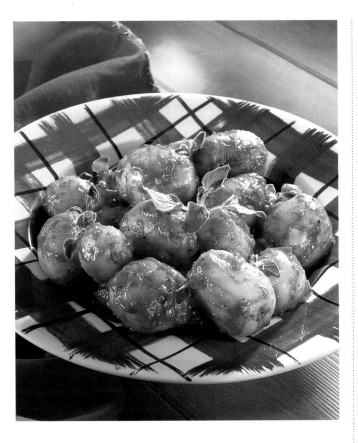

MUSTARD POTATO SALAD

Mustard is an essential ingredient of a good potato salad, and here it holds its own with the other highly flavored ingredients. Small new potatoes are especially delicious, but when they are not available, medium potatoes cut into quarters are fine. Although not vital, making this dish in advance gives the potatoes time to soak up the spicy sauce.

SERVES 4

1¼lb small new potatoes (approximately 20), washed but not peeled
1tbsp English mustard
½tsp hot pepper sauce
4tbsp olive oil

2tbsp tomato paste
1 clove garlic, crushed
2tbsp chopped fresh oregano
1tbsp freshly squeezed lime juice
salt and freshly ground black pepper

Place the potatoes in a saucepan of cold water, bring to a boil, then simmer for 10-15 minutes, or until tender.

Meanwhile, make the mustard dressing. Combine all the remaining ingredients in a small bowl.

Drain the cooked potatoes, rinse under cold water, and drain again. Transfer to a large bowl, pour over the dressing, and mix well.

65

═══ >><< ═══

Mustard Sayings

According to Eric Partridge, the British lexicographer, in his Dictionary of Slang, *the phrase "cut the mustard" means to succeed in performing or accomplishing something, hence to be of importance. He traces the first usage to 1904, when the phrase "up to the mustard," or up to the mark, was also in use. The related expression "to be mustard at" also suggested excellence, but by the 1920s this phrase took on sexual connotations and was altogether more suggestive.* The Dictionary of American Slang, *however, maintains that "cut the mustard" entered the English language in the early 1900s from Philadelphia, where it was said that "groups have special vested interests. And that's not gonna cut the mustard."*

CRUNCHY COLESLAW

Although caraway seeds normally have an intense flavor, their effect in this recipe is tamed by the presence of the mustard. If the coleslaw is allowed to stand, however, the caraway could eventually dominate as the strength of mustard weakens with time. Therefore, you may wish to reduce the quantity of caraway seeds by one teaspoon if you make the coleslaw several hours in advance.

SERVES 4

¼ red cabbage, roughly chopped
¼ white cabbage, roughly chopped
2 carrots, grated
2 sticks celery, chopped

½cup roughly chopped pecans
3tbsp sour cream
2tbsp plain yogurt
2tsp caraway seeds
1tbsp English mustard
2tsp honey

Put the red and white cabbage, the grated carrots, chopped celery and chopped pecans into a large bowl and mix well.

Combine the remaining ingredients, pour onto the vegetables and pecans, and mix thoroughly.

DRESSING & SAUCES

W̲HEN USED IN DRESSINGS AND SAUCES, MUSTARD PLAYS
AN IMPORTANT PART IN THE RECIPE AS IT NOT ONLY PROVIDES FLAVOR
BUT ALSO ACTS AS A THICKENER.

1. C̲ILANTRO D̲RESSING
This fragrant, summery dressing will enhance any salad.

1tbsp whole grain mustard
5tbsp olive oil
2tbsp raspberry wine vinegar
2tbsp roughly chopped fresh
 cilantro, plus extra for garnish
freshly ground black pepper

Combine all the ingredients in a bowl and serve with any salad selection.

2. H̲ERB AND M̲USTARD D̲RESSING
A versatile salad dressing for all occasions.

2tsp whole grain mustard
4tbsp hazelnut oil
2tbsp tarragon vinegar
1tbsp finely chopped fresh tarragon
salt and freshly ground black pepper

Combine all the ingredients in a bowl and serve with a selection of salad ingredients.

3. S̲PICY D̲RESSING
If this dressing is made a few days in advance, its piquancy intensifies.

3tbsp olive oil
1tbsp white wine vinegar
1tsp chili powder
1tsp mustard powder
1 small red chili pepper,
 finely chopped
1 clove garlic, crushed
1tbsp fresh lime juice
freshly ground black pepper

Place all the ingredients in a jar and shake well until combined.

4. Mustardy Hollandaise Sauce

In this sauce, which is traditionally served with fish, the mustard acts as a stabilizer to prevent curdling.

2 eggs, yolks only
2tsp vinegar or lemon juice
1 stick butter, cut into small pieces
2tsp mustard powder
salt

Place the egg yolks and 1 teaspoon of the vinegar or lemon juice with 1 tablespoon of water in a double boiler or in a bowl set over a pan of simmering water (the bowl must not touch the water). Whisk the ingredients together until the yolks just begin to thicken and the mixture clings to the whisk when it is lifted from the bowl. Continue whisking, adding the butter to the bowl 1 piece at a time, making sure each piece is thoroughly incorporated before adding the next.

When all the butter is incorporated and the sauce is thick and creamy, add the mustard powder, salt to taste, and the remaining teaspoon of vinegar or lemon juice.

5. All-Purpose Mustard Sauce

This all-rounder goes well with all meat and vegetable dishes.

2tbsp butter
1½ tbsp flour
1 cup milk
2tsp mustard powder, or 1tbsp Dijon
  mustard
salt and freshly ground black pepper
2tbsp light cream, optional

Melt the butter in a saucepan over a high heat. Stir in the flour and cook for 1 minute. Reduce the heat and pour in the milk gradually, stirring as you pour to prevent lumps from forming. Add the mustard, salt and freshly ground black pepper, and the cream, if using. Bring the mixture to a boil, then serve.

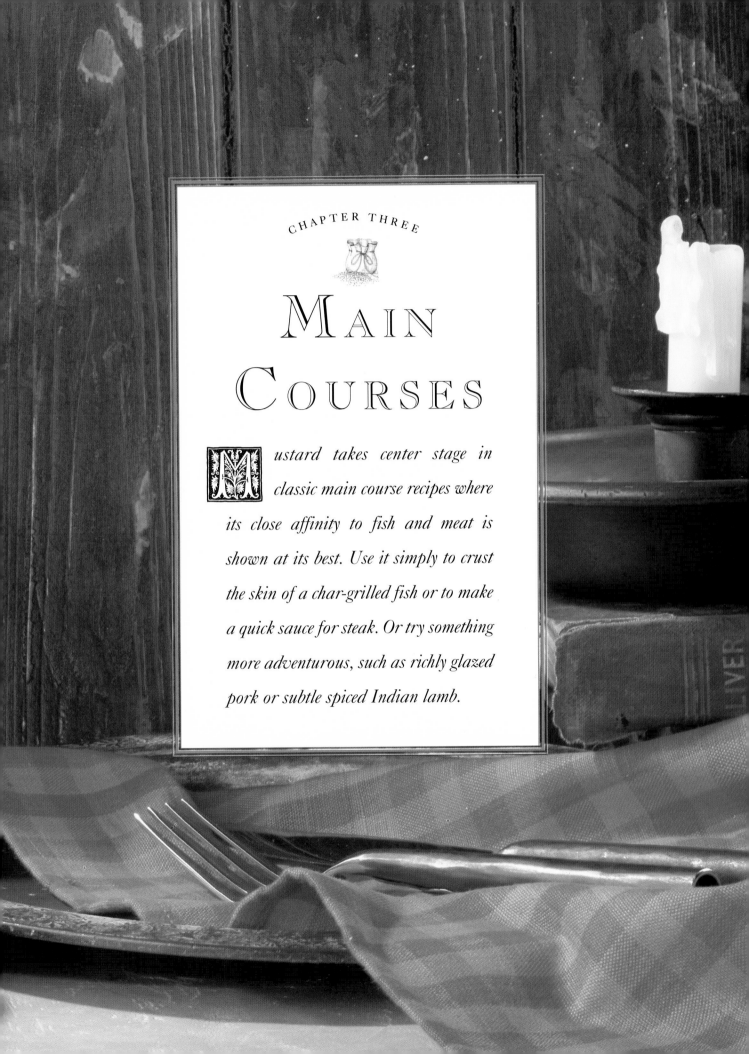

CHAPTER THREE

MAIN COURSES

Mustard takes center stage in classic main course recipes where its close affinity to fish and meat is shown at its best. Use it simply to crust the skin of a char-grilled fish or to make a quick sauce for steak. Or try something more adventurous, such as richly glazed pork or subtle spiced Indian lamb.

MAIN COURSES

The versatility of mustard as a flavoring is seen at its best in main course dishes. It can be used to marinate, to baste, to season, to coat, to stuff, and to sauce, or maybe eaten simply as part of a relish alongside a finished dish.

Many cuisines feature recipes for various meats cooked in mustard-flavored sauces, ranging from those for rabbit and chicken, such as lapin Dijonnaise, *to much stronger flavored kidneys and cuts of beef.*

Sausages, however well seasoned, lack a certain something without mustard to eat with them, and the famous American hot dog, usually a mix of pork and beef, is invariably served with a large squirt of mustard. Germany has dozens of sausage specialties eaten hot with mustard and steaming mounds of sauerkraut or mashed potatoes all washed down with delicious German beer.

Mustardy mayonnaise is delicious with many foods, from simple baked potatoes to a warm salad of baby leeks.

>>>>>>>><<<<<<<

From Chronique D'Angleterre, *late fifteenth century*

FINGER-LICKING SPARE RIBS

These ribs are quite simply delicious! For crispy ribs, cook them in the oven without basting. If you prefer moister ribs, either grill or bake them, basting several times with the marinade during the cooking. The ribs can also be cooked on a barbecue.

SERVES 4

12 spare ribs (about
　2-3lb)
MARINADE
⅓ cup soy sauce
¼ cup rice vinegar
4 cloves garlic, crushed
1in piece fresh root, grated

2tsp chili powder
1 lime, juice only
2tbsp whole grain mustard
1 cup dried apricots, soaked in
　hot water for 10 minutes if
　necessary (see packet
　instructions)
¼ cup soft brown sugar

Place all the marinade ingredients, except for the soft brown sugar, in a food processor and process to a smooth purée. Mix in the sugar carefully, but do not blend as this would make the marinade too runny.

　Place the ribs side by side in a shallow dish, in a single layer if possible, and pour the marinade out making sure the ribs are evenly coated. Cover and place in the refrigerator for 24-48 hours to marinate, the longer the better. Turn the ribs several times while marinating.

　Remove the ribs from the refrigerator at least 30 minutes before cooking. Heat the oven to 400°F, if you are baking the ribs.

　Remove the ribs from the marinade, reserving the marinade for basting if desired. For crispy ribs, bake them in the oven for 30-40 minutes. For moist ribs, bake them in the oven for 15-20 minutes until brown, basting several times with the reserved marinade; alternatively broil them for 20 minutes, turning occasionally and basting several times.

　Serve the ribs whole or cut them into 2½-inch pieces using a meat cleaver.

⟫⟫⟫⟫⟫

A Plowman's Lunch

Plowing was hard, physical work, and the farm worker spent the whole, sometimes cold and wet, day in the fields. For these plowmen, mustard was an invaluable part of their lunch-on-the-job, as it provided them with inner warmth.

PORK TENDERLOIN *glazed in* SUGAR *and* MUSTARD

Nothing is simpler to cook than traditional roast pork, but a coating of sweetened mustard cleverly elevates to culinary heights what might otherwise have been a commonplace dish. What is more, this recipe means that the crackling can be enjoyed as a consequence, by cooking it separately. Serve it with a selection of vegetables such as Potato Gratin (page

SERVES 4

2lb pork loin or boneless leg or
　shoulder, with skin if
　possible
vegetable oil for coating

2tbsp English mustard
¼ cup brown sugar
1½tsp clear honey
freshly ground black pepper

92), Carrots Sautéed with Cumin and Cilantro (page 92) or Golden Parsnip Mousse (page 98).
Heat the oven to 350°F.

　To make the cracking, carefully remove the skin with a layer of fat from the pork using a knife, and cut it into ½-inch wide strips Brush the crackling with oil and sprinkle with salt and place it on a baking sheet.

　In a bowl, combine the mustard, sugar and honey with salt and freshly ground black pepper to form a spreadable mixture. Make several incisions along the pork and rub the mixture all over it and into the incisions.

　Place the pork in a roasting pan and bake in the pre-heated oven for about 2 hours until cooked. Cover the pork with foil for the last 30 minutes.

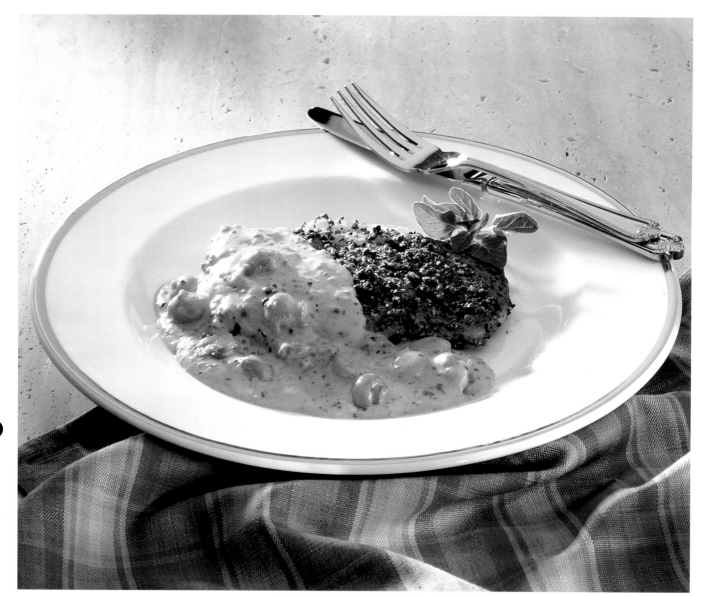

Peppered Steak *with* Mustard Sauce

Creamy mustard sauce, fortified with brandy, is an inspired and luxurious addition to the classic marriage of pepper and steak. Prepared in seconds, this is nonetheless a sophisticated dish that bursts with flavor.

SERVES 4

4tbsp mixed peppercorns,
    crushed
4 sirloin steaks
2tbsp olive oil
1 cup button mushrooms,
    halved

6tbsp heavy cream
5tbsp brandy
2tbsp English or whole grain
    mustard

Press the crushed peppercorns onto both sides of the steaks. Heat the oil in a large skillet and add the steaks, in two batches if necessary. Cook for 2½ minutes each side for a rare steak, 4 minutes each side for medium, or 6 minutes each side for well done.

Remove the cooked steaks from the pan and keep warm. Add the mushrooms to the same pan, scraping up any bits of peppercorn, and fry for 4 minutes, stirring frequently. Pour in the cream and brandy, add the mustard and mix well, gently heating the cream through without allowing it to boil.

Serve each steak with some sauce poured over the top.

SPICY INDIAN LAMB

Marinated in a spicy paste for one to two days, then roasted for several hours and served with a heavily spiced sauce, this is a delicious, if unusual, alternative for a traditional leg of lamb. The tasty sauce is very versatile and can be used, without the added meat juices, with many other dishes. Chapatis (page 106) go well with this dish.

SERVES 4

2½-3lb leg of lamb, trimmed
 of fat
4tbsp vegetable oil
MARINADE
½ cup white wine
2 cloves garlic
1in piece fresh ginger root,
 peeled and roughly chopped
1 green chili pepper, seeded and
 roughly chopped
1 onion, roughly chopped
2tsp yellow mustard powder
1tsp ground coriander
1tbsp mixed peppercorns,
 crushed
1tsp ground cumin
1tsp ground cinnamon

SAUCE
1tbsp vegetable oil
2 shallots, finely chopped
2tsp black mustard seeds
1 small green chili pepper,
 seeded and finely
 chopped
2 cloves garlic, crushed
½in piece fresh ginger root,
 peeled and thinly sliced
½tsp ground turmeric
½tsp ground cumin
½tsp ground coriander
7½oz can chopped tomatoes
1tbsp tomato paste
½ -1 cup white wine,
 according to taste
½ lime, juice only
2tbsp finely chopped fresh
 cilantro

Place all the marinade ingredients in a food processor and purée until smooth. Using a sharp, pointed knife, make several incisions in both sides of the leg of lamb; this will assist the marinating process. Place the lamb in a large dish and pour the marinade over the lamb, rubbing it in. Cover with plastic wrap and place in the refrigerator to marinate for 24-48 hours. Turn the lamb and baste it with the marinade at least twice a day.

Remove the lamb from the refrigerator an hour before cooking to allow it to reach room temperature. Heat the oven to 400°F.

Remove the lamb from the marinade, reserving the marinade. Heat the oil in a large roasting pan, place it on a burner and brown the lamb on all sides. Pour over the reserved marinade, cover the pan with a lid or foil (making sure it does not come into contact with the meat), and roast in the oven for 1 hour. Reduce the temperature to 325°F and cook for a further 2 hours.

Take the lamb out of the oven and set aside to cool slightly. Then transfer the lamb to a warmed serving dish, reserving any meat juices. Strain the juices and skim off any

fat: allow the juices to settle before spooning or pouring off the top layer of fat.

To make the sauce, heat the oil in a skillet over medium heat and gently sauté the shallots for 2-3 minutes until soft. Add the mustard seeds, chili pepper, garlic and ginger and saute for a further 2 minutes. Stir in the turmeric, cumin and ground coriander. Then add the chopped tomatoes, tomato paste, white wine and any reserved meat juices. Cook over a low heat for few minutes until the sauce has reduced slightly. Stir in the lime juice and cilantro leaves and heat through.

Either carve the lamb at the table and serve the sauce separately or carve it in the kitchen and spoon the sauce over the slices of meat.

>>>>>>>><<<<<<<<

MUSTARD MEDLEY

ALL TRUE AFICIONADOS WILL FIND THIS A SURE-FIRE WAY OF WINNING CONVERTS TO THEIR
MUSTARD PASSION. ESSENTIALLY A SELECTION OF BOUGHT MUSTARDS ENLIVENED WITH ADDED INGREDIENTS AND
SERVED WITH COOKED MEATS, THIS IS A GREAT IDEA FOR AN INFORMAL SUPPER PARTY, BUFFET OR BARBECUE.

For the main food you can mix spare ribs, chicken drumsticks, sausages or burgers. Allow two of each per person. Broil the meats under a medium heat; the ribs and chicken drumsticks (with the skin kept on) should first be brushed with olive oil. (You could also try the rib recipe on page 72.) Grilled and roasted vegetables, too, can benefit from a mustard or two to bring out their flavors. Arrange the cooked meats and vegetables on large serving platters with the bowls of mustard scattered around.

All the mustards described here can be made on the day of use and require no curing to develop their flavors. However, for convenience they can also be prepared in advance and will keep for a couple of weeks in the refrigerator. You can vary or augment the selection with your own choice of purchased mustards.

1. GARLIC MUSTARD

5tbsp French mustard
1 head garlic, roasted (see note right)
freshly ground black pepper
1 shallot, very finely chopped

2. OLIVE MUSTARD

5tbsp Dijon mustard
15 stoned black olives,
  finely chopped
1tbsp olive paste
1tbsp extra virgin olive oil

3. GINGER AND CORIANDER MUSTARD

5tbsp whole grain mustard
1cm • ½in piece fresh ginger root, very
  finely chopped
handful cilantro leaves, finely chopped
1 clove garlic

4. DILL MUSTARD

5tbsp American mustard
1tbsp sour cream
2tbsp freshly chopped dilll
freshly ground black pepper

5. SUN-DRIED TOMATO MUSTARD

5tbsp Dijon mustard
45g • 1½oz sun-dried tomatoes in olive
  oil, drained and puréed
1tbsp finely chopped fresh tarragon
  leaves, or 2tsp dried tarragon

To make the mustards, combine the ingredients in a small bowl.
Note: To roast the garlic head for the garlic mustard, wrap the whole garlic in foil and bake in the oven at 400°F for 30 minutes. Remove from the oven, unwrap, and carefully squeeze out the softened garlic from each clove and mix together with the other ingredients.

77

PAN-FRIED COD *with* CAPER *and* MUSTARD SAUCE

This simple-to-prepare dish bursts with flavor. The coarse grain mustard adds bite and helps thicken the sauce, while the black mustard seeds lend earthiness. Serve with wedges of freshly cut lime to squeeze over the fish.

SERVES 4

4 cod steaks or fillets	2tsp black mustard seeds
¼ cup all-purpose flour, seasoned with salt and pepper	1tbsp coarse grain mustard
	2tbsp chopped fresh cilantro
3tbsp olive oil	4tbsp olive oil
2tbsp capers (about 40)	1 lime, juice only
¼ cup stoned green olives, chopped	freshly ground black pepper

Dust the cod pieces with the seasoned flour. Heat the oil in a skillet over a medium heat and shallow-fry the fish for 5 minutes.

Meanwhile, mix together the remaining ingredients to make the sauce. Turn the fish over in the pan and pour the sauce over the fish. Continue to saute for a further 5 minutes, or until the fish is cooked through.

>>>>>>>> <<<<<<<<

PASTA *with* ROASTED PEPPERS *and* WILD MUSHROOMS

Wild mushrooms add a distinctive rich flavor to this dish. If you cannot find any, you can use cultivated mushrooms, but the result will be slightly less intense. It is well worth the effort of removing the bitter skins from the peppers. The amount of mustard you include will depend on your personal taste. Add a little at a time, mixing well and tasting. Serve with a salad and an Italian Country Loaf (page 111).

SERVES 4

1 red sweet pepper
1 yellow sweet pepper
½lb bow pasta (farfalle)
1tbsp butter
freshly ground black pepper
1tbsp olive oil
1 small onion, finely chopped

½ cup wild mushrooms,
  such as chanterelle or ceps,
  wiped clean and torn into
  pieces
1 cup chestnut mushrooms,
  wiped clean and quartered
1 cup light cream
2-4tsp whole grain mustard
salt

Heat the broiler to hot and place the peppers under it to blacken the skins. Turn them regularly to make sure all the skin is blackened. Carefully remove them from the broiler, place them in a plastic bag, and seal. Leave for 5-10 minutes. Once the peppers have cooled sufficiently, remove the skins, deseed, and slice.

Cook the pasta in plenty of boiling water. Drain, reserving 1 tablespoon of the cooking liquid. Transfer the pasta to a warmed serving dish, adding the butter and plenty of freshly ground black pepper. Keep warm.

Heat the oil over a medium heat and add the onion. Saute gently for 5 minutes until soft. Add the peppers and cook for a further minute. Add the mushrooms and mix well with the peppers and onions. Cook gently, covered, for 4 minutes. Pour in the cream, stir in the mustard and salt to taste, adding plenty of black pepper. Cook for a further minute to allow the cream to heat through.

Pour the sauce over the pasta, adding a little of the reserved cooking liquid if the pasta has become too dry.

>>>>>>>> <<<<<<<<

LEMON *and* MUSTARD MACKERAL

80

Mustard, especially the wholegrain variety, seems to have a special affinity with mackerel, and this recipe uses plenty of it. Tie string around each fish to keep it closed and hold the stuffing in place during cooking. You can use any kind of string, the more rustic-looking the better for a "peasant" effect, but make sure it is a natural fiber and not plastic. Serve the fish with the string in place and provide scissors for snipping.

SERVES 4

2tbsp wholegrain mustard	2tbsp capers (about 40)
2tsp hot pepper sauce	¼ cup stoned black olives,
4 whole mackerel or trout,	chopped
gutted and deheaded	1tbsp chopped fresh sage, or
1 lemon, grated rind and 2tbsp	1tsp dried sage
juice only	salt and freshly ground black
½ cup fresh bread crumbs	pepper

Heat the oven to 400°F.
Mix the wholegrain mustard with the hot pepper sauce. Wash the fish and pat dry. Open the fish out flat, flesh side down, and press your fingers hard down along the backbone to release it. Turn the fish over and carefully remove the backbone. Spread the mustard mixture over the flesh.
Combine the remaining ingredients in a bowl to make a stuffing. Divide the stuffing into four parts and spread over the fish. Close up the fish and tie each one with string. Place on a greased baking sheet and bake in the oven for 20 minutes, or until the fish is cooked through.

HONEY-MUSTARD SAUSAGES

The sweet, spicy sauce in this dish livens up what otherwise might be very ordinary fare. A neighbor suggested slitting the sausages because he wanted to get more of the tangy sauce onto the sausages when eating them. Mashed sweet potato would make an excellent accompaniment.

SERVES 4

2tbsp honey	4tbsp soy sauce
2tbsp English mustard	12 pork or beef sausages

Mix the English mustard, honey, and soy sauce together in a bowl.
Prick each sausage and cook either by sautéing or broiling. When the sausages are three-quarters cooked, remove them and carefully slit them down one, side leaving ½ inch uncut at each end. Spoon 1-2 teaspoons of the honey and mustard sauce into each sausage and finish cooking them.
Meanwhile, warm the remaining honey and mustard sauce over a low heat. Remove the cooked sausages carefully without squeezing out any sauce and serve with the heated sauce.

Hot and Sweet

When honey is combined with mustard, such as in making barbecue sauces, marinades and bastes, it adds a subtle sweetness that rounds off the hot flavor, giving it a new dimension. But the honey must be used judiciously so that it does not overpower the taste of the mustard.

>>>>>>>> <<<<<<<<

MEDITERRANEAN SHRIMP PILAF

The inclusion of mustard in a Mediterranean dish is unusual, but here it adds a new dimension to a traditional recipe. The mustard flavor itself is very subtle, influencing the overall taste. Adding another teaspoon of mustard at the last stage of preparation will give more bite to the dish.

SERVES 4

2tbsp olive oil
2 cloves garlic, crushed
1 onion, sliced
2-3tsp coarse grain mustard
1 cup basmati or other long-grain rice
½lb tomatoes, chopped
½ lb shelled cooked shrimp

1tbsp chopped fresh oregano, or 1tsp dried oreganó
½ cup crumbled fetta cheese
½ cup stoned black olives, roughly chopped
1tbsp chopped fresh parsley, or 1tsp dried parsley
salt and freshly ground black pepper

Heat the oil in a large saucepan and gently sauté the garlic and onion for 3 minutes. Stir in 2 teaspoons of the mustard, add the rice and cook for 1 minute more. Add the tomatoes with 1½ cups of water, bring to a boil, then reduce the heat to low and simmer, covered, for 10 minutes without stirring.

Add the shrimp and oregano and cook for a further 5 minutes, or until the rice is tender, adding additional water if the rice becomes too dry.

Stir in the fetta cheese, chopped olives and parsley. Season, adding 1 extra teaspoon of mustard if you like. Remove from the heat and leave for 5 minutes before serving to allow the cheese to melt slightly.

RABBIT *with* MARJORAM *and* MUSTARD

Rabbit cooked with mustard is a classic French dish. The amount of mustard used here is deliberately imprecise, leaving the final decision to personal taste. This recipe works equally well with chicken (use four chicken breasts or eight small pieces) and makes a great dinner party dish.

81

SERVES 4

4tbsp flour for dusting
salt and freshly ground black pepper
1 rabbit (about 2lb), divided into 8 portions
3tbsp vegetable oil
4 small onions or medium shallots, quartered

4 slices bacon, roughly chopped
1pt chicken broth
1¼ cups dry white wine
handful fresh marjoram leaves
1tbsp arrowroot
7tbsp heavy cream
1½-2tbsp Dijon mustard

Season the flour with salt and pepper and dust each portion of rabbit with it. Heat the vegetable oil in a large covered casserole dish over a medium heat and gently sauté the onion or shallot quarters for 4-5 minutes. Remove the onions from the casserole with a slotted spoon and set aside.

Add the rabbit pieces and chopped bacon to the casserole dish and brown on all sides. Return the onions, pour in the chicken broth and white wine, and add the marjoram leaves. Simmer with the lid on for about 1-1½ hours until the rabbit is tender. Remove the rabbit pieces to a heated serving dish and keep warm.

Mix the arrowroot with 1 tablespoon of water and add to the rabbit cooking juices. Increase the heat and boil the juices for about 5 minutes to reduce by about a quarter. Reduce the heat, stir in the cream and Dijon mustard and season. Cook for a further 1 minute until the cream is heated through. Pour onto the rabbit portions and serve.

Traditional Roast Chicken
with Chestnut Stuffing
and Grape Gravy

Mustard adds an extra dimension to the chestnut stuffing of this perennial favorite, a theme that is carried over into the accompanying gravy.

SERVES 4

¼ cup butter
1 small onion, finely chopped
1 stick celery, finely chopped
½ cup fresh bread crumbs
½ cup cooked or canned
    chestnuts, roughly chopped
2tsp mustard powder
1tbsp finely chopped fresh
    parsley, or 1tsp dried
    parsley

1 qt chicken or
    vegetable broth
1 chicken (about 3½-4lb)
1tsp ground arrowroot
½ cup light cream
1tbsp wholegrain mustard
½ lb white grapes, halved and
    seeded
salt and freshly ground black
    pepper

Heat the oven to 375°F.

Melt the butter in a saucepan over medium heat. Add the chopped onion and celery and cook for 4-5 minutes until soft. Add the bread crumbs, chestnuts, mustard powder, parsley and enough broth to moisten the mixture.

Stuff the chicken with half the mixture. Make balls with the remaining stuffing and set aside. Place the chicken in a roasting pan, pour 2 pints of broth around it and season. Bake the stuffed chicken in the preheated oven for about 1½ hours, until the juices run clear. Baste occasionally during cooking with the broth and juices. Add the stuffing balls to the pan for the final 20 minutes. Remove the cooked chicken and the stuffing balls to a warm serving dish and allow to rest.

Meanwhile skim the fat from the cooking juices and place the roasting pan over a high heat. Add the arrowroot and boil rapidly until thickened and slightly reduced, adding additional stock if there is not enough liquid. Pour in the cream, add the mustard and bring back to a boil. Finally, add the grapes, season and gently heat through.

Serve the roast chicken accompanied by the stuffing balls and grape gravy.

Love Potions

Ever since there was love, there have been love potions, with a most successful use of herbal aphrodisiacs portrayed in Shakespeare's A Midsummer Night's Dream. *And, if you are inclined to believe in the power of natural remedies, then a love potion might still lend a helping hand. The mustard plant is a crucial ingredient: used throughout history as a symbol of fertility because of its ability to reproduce on such a prodigious scale, it is also prized for its ability to withstand even the most unfriendly conditions (mustard seeds can lie dormant in the soil for up to a hundred years and still remain viable).*

Both of these qualities make it invaluable in a love potion. Try this potent concoction of herbs and see how the recipient of your passion reacts .

A PINCH OF FENNEL SEEDS (NOT ONLY AN APHRODISIAC BUT ALSO SYMBOLIC OF FLATTERY)

THREE MUSTARD FLOWERS

A SPRIG OF ROSEMARY (AN ANCIENT WEDDING SYMBOL, AND SIGNIFIER OF REMEMBRANCE)

A SPRIG OF LAVENDER (A TRADITIONAL TOKEN OF AFFECTION)

A FOUR-LEAFED CLOVER (A TOKEN FOR LUCK)

Lightly crush the fennel seeds in a pestle and mortar and then infuse them in boiling water with the other ingredients for 10 to 15 minutes. Strain the mixture and discard the herbs. The remaining liquid should then be drunk as a tea.

83

Mustards to Make

>>>>>

The following recipes show you how to make your own delicious mustards. Use them to accompany meat and cheese or in sauces, dressings, soups and stews.

>>>>>

Mustards are easy to mix. Those featured here all use freshly ground seeds which require a few minutes soaking to release the flavors. Once mixed they can be spooned into jars, small bowls, or small pots, then tightly covered and stored in the refrigerator for at least two to three weeks to allow their flavors to develop. They are then ready to use. All the mustards given here should keep in a cool, dark place for up to one year, but if they are continually re-opened and closed, they will begin to lose their pungency and taste blander after six months. If a stored mustard becomes too thick, add a few drops of water.

Mustard seeds can be ground using a pestle and mortar or, if you have one, a coffee grinder that you keep especially for spices. The seeds are finely ground to release all the flavor, except where a coarse or chunky texture is required.
The same method can be used for all these mustards:
Place the ground mustard seeds in a bowl, add enough water to moisten them and leave for 10 minutes.

Place the soaked ground mustard seeds in a food processor with the remaining ingredients and blend thoroughly.

Spoon the mustard into a jar, or small pot, cover tightly, and leave for at least 2 weeks in the refrigerator before opening.

Hot Chili Mustard

The hot chili flavor of this mustard is not apparent at first, but then it hits you in the back of the throat with a real wham. It is great with hot dogs, burgers, steaks and strong, mature cheeses. Try rubbing some into the skin of chicken breasts before grilling to give an extra kick. For smooth blending, add the olive oil with the blender in motion.

1tbsp yellow mustard seeds, finely ground
1tbsp brown mustard seeds, finely ground
3 small dried red chili peppers, very finely chopped
1tbsp mustard powder
1tsp salt
1tbsp sugar
3tbsp red wine vinegar
2tbsp olive oil

PINEAPPLE AND CHILI MUSTARD

A fruity, fairly cool mustard, this is excellent for those who like the taste of mustard but cannot take the heat. It is well suited to fish, duck and steak. Add a spoonful of mayonnaise or sour cream and you have a great party dip. If the mixture is too thick, add a tablespoon of the reserved pineapple juice.

3tbsp mustard powder
1tsp chili powder
¼ lb roughly chopped pineapple, fresh or canned, drained with 1tbsp juice reserved if canned
1tbsp sherry
1tsp salt
1tsp dried oregano
1tsp dried thyme

CRUNCHY CRITUS MUSTARD

When grinding the seeds for this recipe, do so for a few seconds only. The coarsely ground seeds combined with the zest of the fruits will give the mustard a lovely crunchy texture. Use it with vegetables, fish and pork, or in marinades and dressings. The mustard seeds are left to stand in citrus juice for one week to allow them to absorb more of the flavors.

2tbsp yellow mustard seeds, coarsely ground
2tbsp brown mustard seeds, coarsely ground
1 lemon; zest and juice only
1 lime; zest and juice only
2tbsp soft brown sugar

HORSERADISH MUSTARD

If you like your mustard really hot, this is the one for you. It makes a fantastic accompaniment to sausages and mature cheeses as well as – naturally – traditional roast beef.

2tbsp horseradish sauce
4tbsp mustard powder
2tsp sugar
1tsp salt
4tbsp olive oil

Place all the ingredients in a food processor with 2 tablespoons of water and blend thoroughly.

Spoon the mustard into small jars or pots and cover tightly. It will be ready to use in 2 weeks.

CRUNCHY CITRUS MUSTARD
This is a great all-round mustard with a fair amount of heat. Try stirring it into rice dishes or soups just before serving to give extra flavor.

2tbsp yellow mustard seeds, finely ground
2tbsp brown mustard seeds, finely ground
1tbsp fresh parsley, or 2tsp dried parsley
1tbsp fresh thyme, or 2tsp dried thyme
1tbsp fresh oregano, or 2tsp dried oregano
1 clove garlic, roughly chopped
4tbsp white wine vinegar
2tbsp olive oil
1tsp salt
freshly ground black pepper

CHERRY MUSTARD
A perfect accompaniment to pork, smoked meats and duck. If fresh cherries are unavailable, use canned or frozen ones. Although most canned cherries are sweetened with syrup, they can still be used for this summery mustard.

2tbsp yellow mustard seeds, finely ground
2tsp mustard powder
2tbsp raspberry wine vinegar
10 cherries, fresh, canned or frozen, pitted
*   and roughly chopped*
1tsp freshly ground black pepper
1tsp salt
1tbsp cooking sherry

THAI-STYLE MUSTARD
The refreshing, limey flavor of this mustard makes it a useful sandwich spread. As a traditional mustard, it goes well with fish and chicken.

2tbsp brown mustard seeds, finely ground
4tbsp fresh cilantro
2tbsp olive oil
1tbsp mustard powder
1tbsp light brown sugar
1 lime, juice only
2tsp finely chopped lemon grass, or 1tsp
*   dried lemon grass*
2tsp chopped fresh ginger root

TARRAGON MUSTARD

This is a very hot sweet mustard. If it appears too thick, add an additional tablespoon of tarragon vinegar. The mustard marries perfectly with chicken; it also makes a good sandwich spread and can be used in vinaigrette for dressing salads and vegetables.

4tbsp yellow mustard seeds, finely ground
4tbsp chopped fresh tarragon, stems
*   removed, or 1tbsp dried tarragon*
4tbsp tarragon vinegar
1tsp salt
2tbsp sugar
2tbsp mustard powder
1tbsp clear honey

HONEY MUSTARD

Good for keeping in the pantry as a handy baste for meats and fish, this sweet mustard needs a minimum of three weeks for its flavors to develop. Used sparingly, it also makes a tasty sandwich spread.

2tbsp yellow mustard seeds, finely ground
2tbsp mustard powder
3tbsp clear honey
4tbsp white wine vinegar
1tbsp green peppercorns, crushed
1tbsp brown sugar

CHAMPAGNE MUSTARD

This is a great way of using up that last drop of champagne. Alternatively, open a bottle of champagne specially to make the mustard, then sit back and think up a suitable reason to celebrate and finish off the rest of the bottle. If you are feeling slightly less extravagant, you can substitute white sparkling wine. The mustard should be mixed by hand to preserve the champagne bubbles. Serve with poultry, vegetables and cheeses.

3tbsp yellow mustard seeds, finely ground
2tbsp mustard powder
1½tbsp honey
1tsp salt
2tsp sugar
⅓ cup champagne or sparkling wine

CHAPTER FOUR

VEGETABLES

Many varieties of vegetables from across the world are now available throughout the year. No longer just an adjunct to a main course, they can be a meal in their own right. Try aromatic stuffed peppers or a crunchy stir-fry to remind yourself what good partners mustard and vegetables can be.

Vegetables

The Romans used mustard on many vegetable dishes, sprinkling coarse ground seeds on dishes of green beans or beets in oil and vinegar dressing: two ideas which we can copy today. Cooked beets are delicious peeled and dressed while still hot and then eaten before they are totally cold.

Baby beets make a marvelous hot vegetable tossed in butter, lemon juice, and grainy mustard, while large beets baked in the oven are great with a sauce made from crème fraîche, mustard, and a little horseradish to offset the sweetness.

Indian vegetables dishes, either gently or fiercely spiced, often use mustard seeds to great effect. Potato dishes in particular tend to include some of the whole seeds, usually the brown or black type. Fiery little vegetable samosas normally include mustard seed to help spice them, and legumes such as lentils benefit enormously from a touch of mustard seed in any spice mixture added to them.

>>>>>>>> <<<<<<<<

The Ancient Kitchen at Windsor Castle, *W.A. Pyne, 1816*

Colonel Mustard

The word Mustard has been immortalized in Colonel Mustard, the character in the famous board game Clue. Perhaps the originators of the game felt that "Mustard" was an appropriately fiery color to represent this rather hot-tempered looking gentleman.
Appropriately he is seen here in the kitchen.

POTATO GRATIN

Mustard, with a few other well chosen ingredients, really does something for potatoes. This dish is an ideal one to prepare if you are unsure about the time your guests will be arriving or when you will be sitting down to eat. Assemble the gratin, cook for one hour, then reduce the heat to low, and allow the flavors to develop while you wait.

SERVES 4

3 potatoes (about 1½lb), skins on	1tbsp chopped fresh tarragon, or 2tsp dried tarragon
salt and freshly ground black pepper	½ cup heavy cream
1½tbsp Dijon mustard	2 cups chicken or vegetable broth

Heat the oven to 375°F.

Thinly slice the potatoes and layer them in a large, greased gratin dish, seasoning well between the layers.

Stir the Dijon mustard, chopped tarragon and double cream into the broth and pour onto the potatoes. Cover with foil and bake in the oven for 1 hour. If necessary, you can keep the gratin warm on a low heat for a further couple of hours at this stage.

Remove the foil and bake for a further 25 minutes.

CARROTS *sautéed with* CUMIN *and* CILANTRO

This dish takes its inspiration from Indian cooking, where mustard seeds are often combined with spices such as cumin and cilantro to flavor vegetable dishes. If you decide to cook this dish at a time of year when small, young carrots are abundant, use these instead of the large carrots called for and appreciate their heightened sweet flavor.

SERVES 4

3 large carrots (about ¾lb)	1tsp black mustard seeds
2tbsp butter	1tsp cumin seeds
1tbsp vegetable oil	1tsp cilantro seeds
	1tbsp soy sauce

Cut the carrots into three crosswise and each of these pieces into thin strips.

In a sauté pan, heat the butter with the oil over a high heat, then add the mustard, cumin and cilantro seeds. Sauté for about 30 seconds until the seeds begin to pop. Add the carrots, turning them to coat them evenly with the butter and spices, and sauté for 1 minute. Add the soy sauce and continue to cook, covered, for a further 9 minutes until the carrots are barely tender.

>>>>>>>><<<<<<<<

CRUNCHY VEGETABLE STIR-FRY

Stir-frying means cooking the food as quickly as possible to preserve flavor and goodness, which makes it an excellent way of preparing fresh vegetables. The mustard and cumin seeds should be stir-fried first to release their flavors. Serve this crunchy, colorful dish as part of a main meal or as a light lunch.

SERVES 4

1 tbsp vegetable oil
2tbsp black mustard seeds
1tsp cumin seeds
1 clove garlic, crushed
1in piece fresh ginger root, peeled and cut into thin strips

10 radishes, sliced
¼lb snowpeas, topped and tailed
10 baby-on-the-cob
1 cup fresh bean sprouts
4 scallions, shredded

Heat the oil in a wok or heavy skillet over a high heat. Add the mustard seeds and the cumin seeds and stir-fry until they begin to pop. (This will take only 30 seconds or so.) Add the garlic and ginger and stir-fry for a further 20 seconds. Add the radishes, snowpeas, baby cobs, and bean sprouts and stir-fry for 4 minutes. Finally, add the shredded scallions and stir-fry for a further minute.

AROMATIC STUFFED PEPPERS

Using many of the spices traditionally found in Indian cuisine, these stuffed mini-peppers are good as a vegetable accompaniment or buffet dish. If you want a sauce to go with them, the sauce from Spicy Indian Lamb (page 75) goes particularly well.

SERVES 4

vegetable oil for frying
1tbsp black or brown mustard
   seeds
1 green chili pepper, finely
   chopped
1in piece fresh ginger root,
   grated
2 cloves garlic, crushed
½ cup Basmati or long grain
   rice

½ cup white wine
½ cup vegetable broth
1 large potato, diced
1tsp cumin seeds
1tsp ground coriander
1tsp ground paprika
8 small red sweet peppers
handful cilantro leaves, roughly
   chopped

Heat the oven to 375°F.

Heat 1½ tablespoons of the vegetable oil in a large saucepan over a medium-high heat. Add the mustard seeds, chili pepper, ginger and garlic and sauté for 3 minutes until the vegetables are soft. Add the rice, mix well and cook for 2 minutes. Pour in the white wine and bring to a boil. Reduce the heat to low, pour in the broth and cook, covered, for 15 minutes. Lift the lid as little as possible during cooking, but if the rice appears too dry, add more broth.

Meanwhile, pour oil to about 1 inch deep into a skillet and heat high. Add the diced potatoes and sauté for about 12 minutes until golden on all sides. Remove from the pan using a slotted spoon and pour away all but 1 tablespoon of the oil. Heat the oil again until hot, add the cumin seeds, and fry for 30 seconds. Add the ground coriander and paprika and fry for a further 30 seconds. Return the potatoes to the pan and coat in the spices, cooking for a further 1 minute. Remove from the heat.

To prepare the sweet peppers for stuffing, slice off the tops, reserving them, and remove the seeds.

When the rice is cooked, combine with the potatoes and add the cilantro leaves. Fill each pepper with the mixture, replace the top as a lid, and place on a baking sheet. Bake in the oven for 20 minutes.

CILANTRO RÖSTI

Rösti is a Swiss national dish traditionally made just with potatoes and lots of butter. This mustard- and horseradish-flavored variation adds new ingredients all nicely set off by plenty of fresh cilantro. Serve it in wedges as a snack at any time of the day, as an accompaniment to a main meal, or wrap it in foil and take it on a picnic.

SERVES 4

*4 potatoes (about 1lb),
  scrubbed
2 parsnips (about
  ½lb), peeled
1 apple, peeled
2tsp horseradish sauce*

*1tbsp Dijon mustard
3tbsp chopped fresh cilantro
salt and freshly ground black
  pepper
2tbsp butter*

Parboil the potatoes in their skins for 10 minutes. Drain the cooked potatoes and rinse under cold water. Remove the skins and grate the flesh into a large bowl.

Grate the parsnips and apple into the same bowl and mix well. Add the horseradish, mustard and cilantro, and season to taste. Combine all the ingredients thoroughly.

Melt half of the butter in a non-stick skillet, put the rösti mixture into the skillet and press it down with the back of a wooden spoon or spatula to form a flat cake. Cook over a medium heat for 10 minutes, then carefully turn the rösti out onto a plate. Melt the remaining butter in the pan, return the rösti with the uncooked side down and cook for 5-10 minutes. The rösti should be golden brown on both sides.

ORIENTAL STUFFED CABBAGE LEAVES

Added whole to a dish, black mustard seeds impart an earthy savor which in this recipe mingles with the soy and hoisin sauces to give a strong oriental taste. You can serve the stuffed leaves as the vegetable course of a main meal, or on their own as an appetizer.

SERVES 4

*8 large green cabbage leaves
1tbsp olive oil
2tbsp black mustard seeds
2 cloves garlic, finely chopped
1 red sweet pepper, finely diced
8 baby-on-the-cob, each
  chopped into 4 pieces*

*8 shiitake mushrooms, soaked
  in hot water for 30 minutes
  if dried
4tbsp soy sauce
4tbsp hoisin sauce
4tbsp chopped fresh cilantro*

Heat the oven to 350°F.

Blanch the cabbage leaves in boiling water for 5 minutes. Drain and refresh under cold water.

Heat the oil in a saucepan over a high heat, add the mustard seeds, and allow them to pop. Add the chopped garlic and stir-fry for around 30 seconds. Add the sweet pepper, shiitake mushrooms, and baby cobs and stir-fry for a further minute.

Pour in the soy and hoisin sauces. Cover and cook for 5 minutes, adding a little water if the mixture dries out. Remove from the heat and stir in the chopped cilantro.

Divide the mixture between the 8 cabbage leaves, approximately 1 tablespoon per leaf, placing it in the middle of each leaf. Fold in the sides and end of each leaf to make packages and place them, folded sides down, side by side in a greased heatproof dish. Bake for 15 minutes.

Too Much Mustard

These posters, produced by the Mount Horeb Mustard Museum in Wisconsin, demonstrate the vast number and variety of mustards produced internationally, and the challenge to mustard fans of trying all of them! Not only do the types of mustards vary, from wholegrain to smooth and runny, from hot to sweet. Mustard manufacturers take a very different approach to packaging, some opting for traditional Dijon and monastic earthenware pots, while others favor the modern convenience of plastic squeeze tubes and sachets. It is interesting to note that some producers have reverted to using variations of the original Greek name for mustard, as in Senap and Sinappi Senap.

>>>>>>>> <<<<<<<<

GOLDEN PARSNIP MOUSSE

Converting parsnips into a mousse is a perfect way of coaxing out all of their sweet flavor, while the addition of mustard, cream, and paprika enriches it further. Depending on the size of your food processor, you may need to blend the parsnips with the apple in more than one batch.

SERVES 4

2 parsnips (about ¾lb)	salt and freshly ground black pepper
1 apple	2 eggs, lightly beaten
2tsp ground paprika	½ cup heavy cream, chilled
1tbsp Dijon mustard	

Heat the oven to 375°F.

Peel and roughly chop the parsnips and apple, then blend them together in a food processor. Add the paprika, mustard, and seasoning and mix. Lightly beat the eggs and mix these into the mixture. Blend for a further 2 minutes to obtain a smoother mixture. Chill for 30 minutes.

Whip the chilled cream until it forms soft peaks and gently fold it into the chilled parsnip mixture.

Grease a 1 quart heatproof dish and pour in the parsnip mixture. Cover with a sheet of waxed paper and place in a roasting pan half to three-quarters filled with warm water. Bake in the oven for 30 minutes. Carefully remove the paper and cook for a further 10 minutes to brown the top. Serve hot.

LEEKS *with* MUSTARD *and* CHEESE SAUCE

In this filling dish, the delicate flavor of the leeks is admirably set off by the piquancy of the mustard and the bite of good, full-flavored Cheddar cheese. The perfect accompaniment is mashed or baked potato.

SERVES 4

4 large leeks (about 1½lb), trimmed and washed	1¼ cups milk
	1½tbsp coarse grain mustard
6 slices ham, cut in two	¼lb grated Cheddar cheese
3tbsp butter	salt and freshly ground black pepper
3tbsp all-purpose flour	

Heat the oven to 350°F.

Cut each leek into 3 pieces and parboil them in boiling salted water for 3 minutes. Drain them.

Wrap a piece of ham around each leek and place them side by side in a greased ovenproof dish.

Melt the butter in a saucepan over high heat and stir in the flour. Reduce the heat to medium and cook for 30 seconds, stirring frequently. Pour in the milk, stirring well to prevent lumps from forming. Add the coarse grain mustard and three-quarters of the grated cheese and mix well.

Pour the cheese sauce over the leeks, sprinkle the remaining cheese on top, and bake in the oven for 20 minutes.

This charming late nineteenth-century advertisement, produced by Keen's of England, depicts a scene from Shakespeare's As You Like It *in which Celia and Rosalind quiz the Fool, Touchstone.*

ROSALIND
Where learned you that oath, fool?

TOUCHSTONE
Of a certain knight that swore by his honour that they were good pancakes and swore by his honour that the mustard was naught: now I'll stand to it the pancakes were naught and the mustard was good, and yet was not the knight forsworn.

The clever use of selective quotation allows Keen's to suggest that no less a person than Shakespeare was an advocate of their product.

The Mustard Club

In the early twentieth century, the appeal of mustard was waning in Britain, so Colman's responded with a brilliant advertising campaign of a kind never seen before. They asked the S. H. Benson advertising agency to come up with a revolutionary new campaign, which turned out to be hugely successful.

The sides of London buses were used to carry the message "Has father joined The Mustard Club?" The club consisted of a group of fictitious people such as Miss Di Gester (the secretary), Lord Bacon of Cookham, Master Mustard, Lady Hearty and Signor Spaghetti, author of the famous song "O Mostardo Mio." The

RULES of the MUSTARD CLUB

1. **Every member** shall on all proper occasions eat Mustard to improve his appetite and strengthen his digestion.

2. **Every member** when physically exhausted or threatened with a cold, shall take refuge in a Mustard Bath.

3. **Every member** shall once at least during every meal make the secret sign of the Mustard Club by placing the mustard pot six inches from his neighbour's plate.

4. **Every member** who asks for a sandwich and finds that it contains no Mustard shall publicly refuse to eat same.

5. **Every member** shall see that the Mustard is freshly made, and no member shall tip a waiter who forgets to put Mustard on the table.

6. **Each member** shall instruct his children to "keep that schoolboy digestion" by forming the habit of eating Mustard.

The Password of the Mustard Club is

"Pass the Mustard, please."

A bust of the main character of The Mustard Club, Baron de Beef, complete with monocle.

The six crucial rules of the club, displayed with an impressive heraldic device above them.

president was a monocled Baron de Beef and the password was, of course, "Pass the mustard, please," while the motto was "Mustard makyth Methuselahs." The heraldic shield of the club appeared on menus and restaurant cards separate from the campaign itself and helped boost the publicity for Colman's. Much of the success of the campaign was due to Dorothy L Sayers, who worked on it as a copywriter. She is better remembered, however, as the author of detective novels starring the aristocratic sleuth Lord Peter Wimsey. The campaign ran from 1926 to 1933 and spawned many spin-offs such as books, card games, badges, and eight Mustard Club songs. Over 2,000 applications arrived when the offer of a badge was made, and extra jobs were created by Colman's to help meet the extra demand the campaign caused.

The main officers of The Mustard Club, from left to right: Miss Di Gester, Lord Bacon of Cookham, Master Mustard, the Baron de Beef, Signor Spaghetti, and Lady Hearty.

An early full page advertisement from 1926 for The Mustard Club, in mock-serious style. Great efforts were made to make the whole thing appear credible, even if the words were clever nonsense.

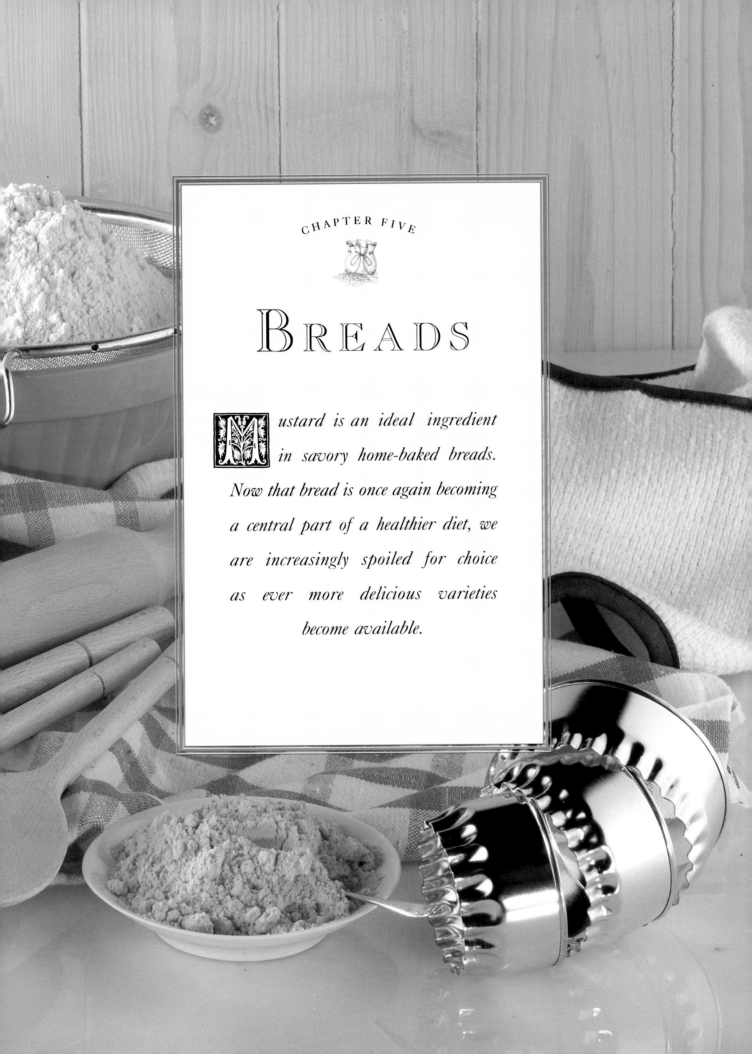

CHAPTER FIVE

BREADS

Mustard is an ideal ingredient in savory home-baked breads. Now that bread is once again becoming a central part of a healthier diet, we are increasingly spoiled for choice as ever more delicious varieties become available.

BREADS

The sandwich gained its name in the eighteenth century. John Montague, the 4th Earl of Sandwich, was an inveterate gambler and rather than withdraw from the gaming tables to eat at the dining table, he preferred to have meat brought to him between slices of bread. This convenient snack became known as a sandwich. No doubt if the meat was beef or pork, a generous dash of freshly made mustard was added. In fact, mustard has become a vital ingredient for both cold roast beef and ham sandwiches, not to mention cheese or even egg mayonnaise. Any food put between two slices of bread has to be well flavored to hold its own. Imagine a toasted cheese and tomato sandwich: perfectly fine if a little dull. Now imagine it spread liberally with good grainy mustard – and it is transformed.

Mustard plays a crucial part in another bread-based dish – toasted cheese or Welsh rarebit. The mustard helps to cut across the richness of the cheese and provides a sharpness and edge which brings the whole thing amazingly to life. Mustard addicts will have their own preferences as to what type it should be; smooth, mild American or fiery British, or maybe even a grainy French one.

>>>>>>>> <<<<<<<<

The Sower, *Jean-François Millet, 1850*

Chapatis *with* Mustard Seeds

Mustards seeds are not normally baked into chapatis (flat, unleavened Indian bread), but here they add a slight crunch. If you cannot find chapati flour, a very fine-textured, low-gluten flour also known as ata flour, you can use equal quantities of all-purpose and wholewheat flours instead. The chapatis can be served with a multitude of Indian dishes; try them with Spicy Indian Lamb (page 75).

MAKES 8

3 cups chapati flour, or 1½ cups
   each of all-purpose and
   wholewheat flour, plus extra
   for dusting
pinch salt
½tsp sugar
5tbsp vegetable oil
2tbsp black mustard seeds
3tbsp butter, melted

Combine the flour, a good pinch of salt, and the sugar in a large bowl. Add half of the vegetable oil and rub into the flour with your fingertips. Gradually add ¾cup warm water, gathering the mixture together, until a soft dough is formed. Add the remaining oil and the mustard seeds and knead for about 2 minutes. Transfer the dough to a floured work surface and knead for a further 5-8 minutes. The dough should stop sticking to the work surface and become soft and pliable. Shape the dough into a ball, place it in a clean bowl, cover with a damp cloth, and set aside for 30 minutes.

Knead the dough for a further minute and divide the mixture into 8 portions. Work on one portion at a time, always keeping the others covered. Roll each portion into a ball, then flatten it with the palm of your hand.

When all portions have been rolled and flattened, heat a heavy-based skillet or griddle over a high heat. Using a rolling pin, roll a flattened portion into an 8-inch circle, place it immediately in the skillet and start rolling the next. Cook each chapati for 2 minutes on the first side, turn it over with a spatula, and cook the second side for 2-3 minutes or until black spots start to appear. Turn the chapati over again and cook until black spots appear on this side, too.

Line a serving dish with paper towels and pile up the chapatis, brushing each one with melted butter as you work. The absorbent paper will prevent the chapatis from becoming soggy.

Onion *and* Rosemary Focaccia

Focaccia is a deliciously moist, round Italian loaf made with olive oil. Wedges of this subtly flavored version make a welcome addition to any meal, whether served hot or cold. Cut into thick slices, it can make a splendid ham sandwich, especially when spread with a herb mustard (page 86).

SERVES 4

4 cups strong white flour
½tsp active dried yeast
1tsp salt
5tbsp olive oil
3tbsp roughly chopped fresh
   rosemary
2tsp black mustard seeds
2tbsp butter
2 red onions, sliced
1tbsp rock salt

Combine the flour, yeast and salt in a large mixing bowl. Heat 1¼cups water until hand-hot and pour into the mixing bowl with 2 tablespoons of the oil, 1 tablespoon of the rosemary, and all the mustard seeds. Mix until the mixture has a dough-like consistency.

Knead the dough on a floured surface for 10-15 minutes. Place on a floured board or in a floured bowl, cover and leave in a warm place (average room temperature will do) for about an hour until it has doubled in size.

Roll out the dough to a 10-inch circle and place on a greased baking sheet. Leave to rise for a further hour. Heat the oven to 450°F.

Heat 1 tablespoon of the oil with the butter in a saucepan. Add the sliced onions and cook gently for 20 minutes, stirring occasionally to make sure the onions remain well coated.

Spoon the onions over the risen dough to cover it. Pour on the remaining 2 tablespoons of oil and scatter over the remaining rosemary with the rock salt. Bake in the oven for 15–20 minutes until golden brown.

FIERY PEPPERONI PIZZA

Mustard, hot pepper sauce, and pepperoni combine to make this pizza hot stuff. The topping also uses passata, a smooth sauce of strained chopped tomatoes, (available in many supermarkets). This recipe makes one large thin and crispy pizza; if you prefer thick-crust pizzas, roll out the dough to 5-inch circles and increase the baking time to about 30–35 minutes.

To make the pizza dough, sift the yeast with the flour into a

SERVES 4

1tsp active dried yeast	*1tbsp yellow mustard powder*
300g • 10oz plain flour	*2tsp hot pepper sauce*
1tbsp olive oil	*250g • 8oz Italian mozzarella*
TOPPING	*cheese, sliced*
120ml • 4floz passata	*20 slices pepperoni sausage*

large bowl. Add ⅝ cup lukewarm water and mix well. Cover and set aside for 30 minutes.

Add the olive oil and knead into a soft dough. Place on a floured work surface and knead for about 10 minutes. Return the dough to a clean bowl, cover and leave in a warm place (average room temperature will do) for 2 hours, or until it has doubled in volume. Heat the oven to 400°F.

Place the dough on a floured work surface and knead for 1 minute. Roll out to make a 12-inch circle. Carefully transfer the pizza base to a greased baking sheet.

For the topping, mix the passata, English mustard, and, hot pepper sauce together and spread over the pizza base. Arrange the mozzarella slices and pepperoni sausage on top. Bake in the oven for 20–25 minutes, until the cheese is melted and the crust is golden.

>>>>>>>> <<<<<<<<

FRESH HERB *and* MUSTARD SCONES

The aroma of freshly baked scones heavy with warmed herbs and tangy mustard is nothing short of irresistible. Perfect for serving with morning coffee or afternoon tea, these savory snacks will quickly vanish. They can also be filled with cheese or ham and taken on a picnic.

MAKES ABOUT 15

2 cups all-purpose flour
1tbsp baking powder
2tsp mustard powder
1tsp salt
3tbsp butter, cut into small pieces
1tbsp finely chopped fresh

herbs, such as parsley, thyme, or oregano, or 2tsp dried herbs
1tsp sugar
1 shallot, finely chopped
freshly ground black pepper
¼ cup milk

Heat the oven to 450°F.

Sift the flour, baking powder, mustard powder, and salt into a large bowl. Rub the butter into the mixture using your fingertips. Add the herbs, sugar, shallot, and black pepper and mix well. Pour in ½ cup of the milk and mix in quickly. If the dough is too stiff, add the extra milk to soften it. Place the dough on a floured surface and knead 4 or 5 times with the heel of your hand. Shape the dough into a circle approximately ⅜-inch thick and, using a pastry cutter, cut into 1¼-inch circles.

Place the circles of dough on a baking sheet and bake in the oven for 10-15 minutes until golden brown. For soft scones, wrap them in a clean dish towel as soon as they are removed from the oven. For crusty scones, place them on a wire rack to cool.

>><<

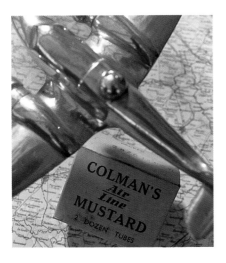

High Flier

So many airline passengers consider that adding a dash of mustard, like adding salt and pepper, is vital to the enjoyment of their meals that mustard producers supply very small tubes especially for airline use.

An Added Kick

As mixing mustard seed with wine or grape must is a traditional way of making mustard, it is not surprising that mustards blend well with alcoholic drinks. An extensive range of mustards with the added dimension of any number of international wines and spirits is now available. Irish whiskey and Jack Daniels add an extra "kick," while sloe gin, made by steeping sloes, the fruit of the blackthorn, in gin sweetened with sugar, produces a uniquely mellow mustard. The addition of Guinness beer makes for a more full-bodied, rounded mustard, while champagne adds a lighter, more delicate flavor.

>>>>>>>> <<<<<<<<

ITALIAN COUNTRY LOAF *with* SAVORY FILLING

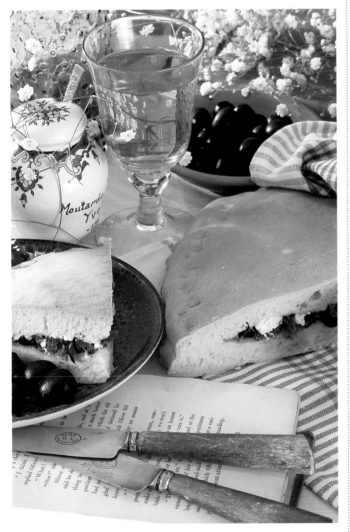

The medley of wonderful tastes stuffed inside this freshly baked bread evokes sun-drenched Mediterranean hillsides. When the loaf is ready it should feel very hard and sound hollow when tapped. Leave it to stand for 10 minutes before slicing and eating it warm. It can also be eaten cold and is ideal for picnics.

MAKES 1 LOAF

1tbsp active dried yeast	*parsley, and thyme, or 1tbsp*
1tbsp salt	*dried mixed herbs*
4 cups strong white flour	*20 black olives, pitted and*
2tbsp olive oil	*roughly chopped*
FILLING	*½ cup sun-dried tomatoes in*
2tbsp Dijon mustard	*olive oil, drained and*
2tbsp roughly chopped mixed	*roughly chopped*
fresh herbs such as oregano,	*2tbsp ricotta cheese*

First make the dough. Heat 1⅛ cups water until it is lukewarm. Pour half into a bowl, sprinkle the yeast over, and leave to stand. Dissolve the salt in the remaining water. Sift the flour into a bowl, make a well in the center, and pour the two liquids into it. Combine the mixture well with a metal spoon. Add the olive oil and mix again. When the ingredients are well combined, place the dough on a floured surface and knead for about 10 minutes. Place the dough in a clean bowl, cover, and leave in a warm place (average room temperature will do) for 1 hour to rise. Heat the oven to 400°F.

Place the dough on a floured surface again and knead for a further 2 minutes. Divide the dough into two and roll out one half to a 10-inch circle.

For the filling, combine the Dijon mustard with the mixed herbs and spread evenly on the rolled-out dough, leaving an uncovered 1-inch border all around. Sprinkle on the chopped olives, sun-dried tomatoes, and ricotta cheese, again leaving the border uncovered.

Roll out the second half of the dough to the same size and place on top of the first. Moisten the edges of the two dough pieces and pinch together. Bake in the oven for 40 minutes, or until the loaf has risen and is golden brown.

111

PARMESAN *and* ALMOND MUFFINS

Parmesan cheese and almonds may seem an odd combination at first sight, but the almonds add crunch and the parmesan sweetness. The generous helping of mustard develops the flavor of the muffins without being too strong itself. These light, little breads are quick and easy to make and are best served warm.

MAKES ABOUT 16 MUFFINS OR 32 MINI MUFFINS

1 cup all-purpose flour	*1 egg*
2tsp baking powder	*½ cup milk*
salt and freshly ground black	*3tbsp butter, melted*
pepper	*2tbsp English mustard*
60g • 2oz freshly grated	*¼ cup flaked almonds*
Parmesan cheese	

Heat the oven to 400°F

Sift the flour, baking powder, and a pinch of salt into a large bowl. Add some pepper and the grated Parmesan cheese.

In another bowl, combine the egg, milk, melted butter, and mustard. Pour the wet ingredients onto the dry ones and mix well.

Spoon the mixture into greased muffin cups and scatter the flaked almonds over the tops. Bake in the oven for 20 minutes until golden brown.

All Boxed Up

The packaging and advertising of mustard has a colorful and well-attested history. For some reason, this quite ordinary product, whether as a yellow powder or a ready-mixed paste, has brought out the best in advertising creativity. Now that mustard is often one product among many in an international food giant's portfolio, the quirky and stimulating packaging and posters have gone, probably forever, but there still remain some wonderful examples of the old-fashioned approach to advertising.

A marvelously robust John Bull strides across the world, delivering Britain's Colman's mustard to its farthest corners. The proud boast "By special appointment to the King" is clearly visible.

Patriotic emblems and symbols have been used to give this mustard plenty of credibility and Britishness. The company must have been a small one and is not very well known.

Fine examples of early Keen's packaging, proving how successful the color scheme of red and yellow was. It was not successful enough, however, to stop it from being swallowed up by its rival Colman's.

A typical piece of nineteenth-century American packaging, with an impressive head of the company's founder, J. R. Watkins. The design is more reminiscent of a medicine than a food package.

Many smaller mustard companies seemed to virtually copy the larger ones when it came to packaging. This design is reminiscent of both Keen's and Colman's, but the rather strange, Chinese-inspired "A" is intriguing.

Another company sensibly packaging its mustard in containers which could be used again. Mustard and some other food products are still sold in reusable containers in France today.

Colman's of Norwich used the bull's head symbol for many years in the early days of its advertising. In Britain, at least, mustard would always be linked with beef.

113

One of the mustard companies of Dijon (1816), draws on the town's history of the condiment to depict a medieval meal, with a toast, no doubt, to "Monsieur Moutarde."

Keen's, at one time probably Britain's best-known British mustard producer, commissioned these powerful graphics to ram home the name of the brand. The use of red and mustard yellow together is eye-catching and memorable.

A simple but striking design for Keen's powdered mustard. The shell symbol remains important and a dash of blue brings the red and yellow to life. Some people claim that the expression "as keen as mustard" comes from this company's name.

TRADE MARK.

KEEN'S

A.D. TRADE MARK 1742

MUSTARD

DOUBLE SUPERFINE
WARRANTED GENUINE

Amora mustards from France have often been packaged in reusable glasses. Here are advertisements for two versions which hardly mention the mustard. One comes in a choice of tempting colors inspired by the "aurora borealis," and the second has a 1950s interpretation of an African design.

CHAUD
COLORÉ
LUMINEUX   *le gobelet* ÉQUATEUR

une nouveauté
AMORA
LA MOUTARDE DE DIJON

AMORA
LA MOUTARDE FORTE QUI RESTE FORTE

PRÉSENTÉ SON VERRE
"BORÉAL"
COLORÉ

ÉLÉGANT VERRE SEMI-CRISTAL EN 3 COLORIS "GIVRÉ": ROSE, VERT, JAUNE

>>>>>>> <<<<<<<

A Savora advertisement from 1937, depicting all kinds of influences of the day, such as film and architecture. The artist's signature is prominent.

A French mustard manufacturer making an "English" mustard seems on the face of it highly unusual. The name might have worked in France, but it is doubtful if it would ever have become popular in Britain.

A moon face – or is he a fiery, devilish mustard seed? These curious packaging labels from the beginning of this century (above and left) come from two of the many less well-known Dijon mustard makers

CHAPTER SIX

PRESERVES

*W*ithout that taste of mustard, pickles and chutneys would lack the zest, heat and color, body and crunch, that the relish gives to preserved mixtures of fruits and vegetables. Humble, homly everyday pickles or subtle and sophisticated chutneys are just some of the many mixtures that benefit from the magical seeds.

PRESERVES

Preserves were once an essential part of every well-stocked pantry cupboard, providing fruits and vegetables for lean winter months. Today they give color and spice to the cook's palette and have become a really creative branch of cooking. Mustard is one of the most popular ingredients and plays an important role in many recipes for pickles, preserves, and chutneys. Generally, vegetables and fruits are pickled by individual type, but mixtures are found, too – such as those displayed in enormous jars in delicatessens with mixed vegetables packed inside with exquisite artistry. A spectacular Italian specialty is mostarda di frutta *from Cremona, containing a variety of preserved fruits such as oranges, figs, plums, apricots, pears, cherries, and slices of pumpkin and melon, flavored with mustard oil in a bitingly hot sweet syrup. It is frequently eaten with the Italian mixed meat dish, bollito misto. Its origin dates from the days when sweet and sour flavors used together were commonplace.*

>>>>>>>> <<<<<<<<

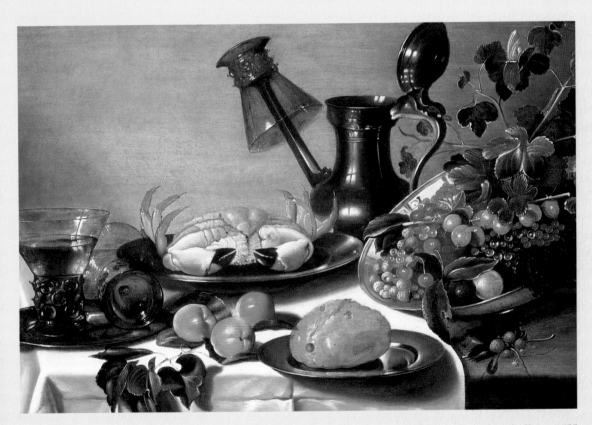

Still life of fruit, *Cornelis Kruys, 1655*

>>>>>>>> <<<<<<<<

SPICY TOMATO RELISH

A superb accompaniment for hamburgers and hot dogs, this relish will also wake up cold meats, enliven broiled chops or cheese, and add surprise to sandwiches. If it is still not hot enough for some tastes, mix in a teaspoon of hot pepper sauce before serving. The relish is ready to eat after one week. Unopened, it will keep for up to three months.

MAKES ABOUT 2 QUARTS

5lb ripe tomatoes, cut into small pieces
5 red onions (about 1lb), thinly sliced
1tbsp salt
1tbsp black mustard seeds
2tsp cumin seeds
4 long dried red chili peppers
2tsp chili powder
2 cups white wine vinegar
1 cup sugar

Place the chopped tomatoes and onion slices in a shallow dish and sprinkle with the salt. Leave overnight.

Using a pestle and mortar or coffee grinder, crush the mustard seeds, cumin seeds and chili peppers.

Drain the tomatoes and onions and place them in a saucepan with the crushed spices, chili powder, white wine vinegar, and sugar. Bring to a boil, then simmer, covered, for 45 minutes, stirring frequently. Remove the lid and simmer for a further 15 minutes.

Spoon the relish into hot, sterilized mason jars, filling them completely and seal.

>><<

The Earliest Mustard

Some of the earliest advice on preparing mustard is given in De Re Rustica, *a treatise on farming and country life, published in twelve books in the first century* A.D. *by Lucius Junius Moderatus, or Columella, a retired Roman legionnaire: "Clean the mustard seeds carefully. Sift it well and wash in cold water. After it is clean, soak, it in cold water two hours. Stir it, squeeze it, and put it into a new, or very clean, mortar. Crush it with a pestle. When it is well ground, put it in the center of the mortar, press and flatten it with the hand. Make furrows in the surface and put hot coals in them. Pour water with saltpeter over these. This will take the bitterness out of the seed and prevent it from molding. Pour off the moisture completely. Pour strong white vinegar over the mustard, mix it thoroughly with the pestle, and force it through a strainer."*

>>>>>>>> <<<<<<<<

ITALIAN PRESERVED FRUITS

Fruit preserved in a mustard-flavored syrup is a specialty of northern Italy. *Mostarda di frutta*, as it is known, is traditionally served with game and poultry. You can experiment with your own combinations of fresh and/or dried fruits; ones that immediately spring to mind are apricots, figs, pineapple, apples, pears, plums, and nectarines. After bottling, store in the refrigerator where it will keep for several months. It is ready to be eaten after two weeks.

MAKES ABOUT 4 CUPS
1⅓ cups sugar
1 cup raspberry wine vinegar
2tsp mustard powder
2tsp yellow mustard seeds
2lb mixed fresh and/or dried fruits cut into bite-sized pieces

Put half of the sugar into a saucepan with 1 cup of water and bring to a boil, stirring frequently and making sure the sugar dissolves. Add the fresh fruits you are using to the syrup and simmer for about 10 minutes until the fruits are tender.

Put the remaining sugar into another saucepan with the raspberry wine vinegar and the mustard powder and seeds. Bring to a boil and simmer for 5 minutes.

Allow both syrups to cool completely; then mix them together and stir in the dried fruits.

Spoon the cooked fruits into hot, sterilized mason jars, making sure that all the fruit is covered by the syrup. Cover and seal.

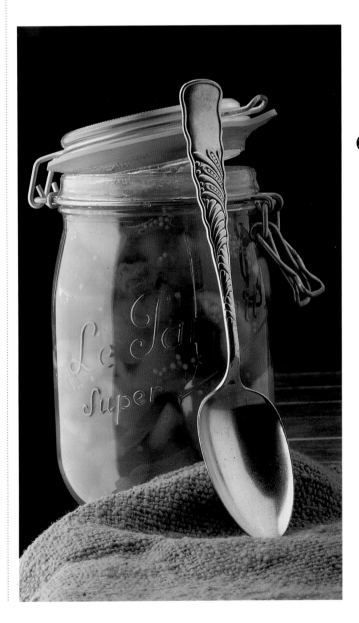

GRAPE AND GINGER CHUTNEY

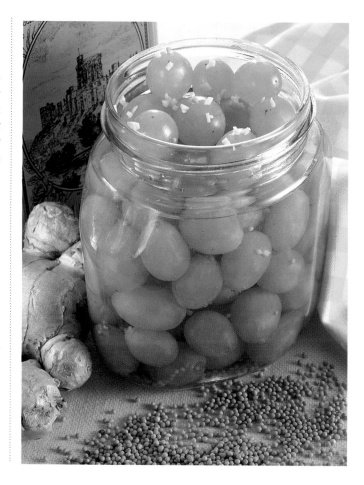

Chutneys were devised in the Indian subcontinent to accompany curries, and this strongly flavored tangy, fruity version carries on the tradition. It is also excellent as a companion to fish, poultry, and game. Store the chutney for at least four weeks before using. Unopened, it will keep for up to one year. If you use white grapes, store in a dark place to prevent discoloration.

MAKES ABOUT 1½ CUPS

2tbsp vegetable oil
1tsp cayenne pepper
4tsp yellow mustard seeds
1lb white or black grapes

2in piece fresh ginger root,
*   peeled and grated*
salt and freshly ground black
*   pepper*
1 cup white wine vinegar

Heat the oil in a saucepan, add the cayenne pepper with the mustard seeds, and fry over a high heat for about 30 seconds.

Add the remaining ingredients, reduce the heat to low and cook, covered, for about 30 minutes. Remove the lid and simmer for a further 10-15 minutes until the mixture has the same consistency as thick chutney.

Pour into hot, sterilized mason jars, cover and seal.

122

—————————— >><< ——————————

Eliza Acton

The daughter of an English brewer, Eliza Acton was the author of Modern Cookery *(1845) and* The English Bread Book *(1857). Both books were enormously popular and influential in Britain in the second half of the nineteenth century. Mrs. Acton included recipes for both mild mustard, mixed with milk and very thin cream, and "an extremely pungent compound, which has many approvers" called Tarter Mustard, a mixture of Durham mustard, strong horseradish vinegar, cayenne or chili vinegar, and tarragon vinegar. Her advice was: "The great art of mixing mustard is to have it perfectly smooth, and of a proper consistency."*

Mustard Pickle

Mustard pickles can be made with almost any combination of crisp vegetables, but matching cucumbers, small white onions, sweet peppers, and cauliflower in varying proportions is a classic recipe. The result is often known as Piccalilli. You can serve this traditional pickle as part of a salad platter or as an antipasto. Keep it for at least three weeks before using. Unopened, it will last for up to three months.

MAKES ABOUT 2 QUARTS

3 small cucumbers, roughly chopped into 1in cubes
1lb small white onions, halved
1 red sweet pepper, diced
1 small cauliflower, or ½ large one, broken into flowerets
2tbsp salt

2¼ cups malt vinegar
1½tsp mustard powder
2tsp yellow mustard seeds
1½tsp cornstarch
1tsp ground turmeric
1tbsp, approximately, cider vinegar
2tbsp sugar

Put the cucumber, onions, sweet pepper, and cauliflower in a bowl. Cover with water, add the salt, and leave to soak for 8 hours.

Drain and rinse the vegetables under cold water to remove the salt, then put them into a saucepan. Pour in enough malt vinegar to almost cover the vegetables and bring to a boil.

Meanwhile, combine the mustard powder, yellow mustard seeds, cornstarch and turmeric in a small saucepan and add approximately 1 tablespoon of cider vinegar, just enough to form a paste.

As soon as the vegetables come to a boil, add the paste and boil for 5 minutes. Add the sugar and boil for a further 3 minutes, or until the sugar has dissolved and the mixture has thickened.

Spoon the pickle into hot, sterilized mason jars, filling them completely. Cover and seal.

123

>>>>>>>> <<<<<<<<

BANANA *and* RAISIN CHUTNEY

A very sweet chutney, this partners strong cheeses, such as mature Cheddar, and cold meats particularly well. Keep the chutney for at least one month before using. Unopened, it will keep for up to two years.

MAKES ABOUT 5 CUPS

1 lemon	crushed
6 bananas (about 2lb including skins), peeled and sliced	1tsp caraway seeds
	3tsp salt
1¼ cups raisins	1tsp ground nutmeg
1tbsp yellow mustard seeds,	5 cups malt vinegar
	1lb sugar

Remove the skin and pith from the lemon. Cut it into ½-inch slices, then cut each slice into quarters.

Put the lemon slices into a saucepan with all the ingredients except the sugar, cover, and bring to a boil. Add the sugar and stir to dissolve it. Simmer for 1½-2 hours, uncovered and stirring occasionally, until the mixture thickens to the consistency of chutney. During the last half hour of cooking, check to make sure that the chutney does not become too dry and burn.

Pour the chutney into hot, sterilized mason jars, filling them completely. Cover and seal.

FRESH CORN RELISH

Corn and mustard are a perfect relish marriage. Because the cooking time of a relish is less than that of a chutney, the vegetable pieces hold their shape and are identifiable in the finished preserve. This relish is ready to use after one week and will keep for up to three months.

MAKES ABOUT 2½ CUPS

⅓ cup sugar	fresh or frozen
1tsp salt	1 small green chili pepper,
1tsp yellow mustard seeds	finely sliced
1tsp mustard powder	1 red sweet pepper, finely diced
1 cup cider vinegar	1 onion, finely chopped
1lb corn kernels,	

Put the sugar, salt, yellow mustard seeds, and mustard powder into a saucepan, pour in the cider vinegar and ½ cup of water, and bring to a boil. Add all the remaining ingredients, bring back to a boil, and simmer, covered, for 45 minutes, stirring frequently.

Remove the lid and simmer uncovered for a further 10 minutes. Increase the heat and boil the mixture rapidly for 5 minutes, or until the mixture is thick.

Spoon the relish into hot, sterilized mason jars, filling them completely. Cover and seal.

>><<

Shipwrecked

An eighteenth-century consignment of mustard and vinegar en route to Russia from France was lost when the ship carrying it was sunk off the Finnish Island of Jurasso. Salvaged in 1979, one of the original mustard pots is now exhibited at the Grey Poupon Mustard Shop in Dijon, France.

General Index

Italics refer to illustration captions.

INDEX *of* RECIPES

ACKNOWLEDGEMENTS

Key: (a) above   (b) below
Jean Pierre Picughot/Image Bank 6, Bodleian Library 7, Mansell Collection 8,
Food & Wine from France Ltd 8 (a), Roger-Viollet 8 (b), Harry Smith
Horticultural Collection 10 (a), Mansell Collection 10 (b), Colman's of
Norwich 11 (a), Mansell Collection 11 (b), Pictor 12–13, Harry Smith
Horticultural Collection 14 (b), Dennis Davis/Ace 15, e.t. Archive 16 (a),
Mansell Collection 16 (b), Roger-Viollet 17 (a & b), 18 (a), Bodleian Library 18
(b), Roger-Viollet 19 (a), Edmund Nagele/Ace 19 (b), Pictor 20, Edmund
Nagele/Ace 21 (a), Colman's of Norwich 21 (b), Mansell Collection 22 (a & b),
Colman's of Norwich 23 (a), Thierry Perrin/Rex Features 23 (b), Culpeper Ltd
24, e.t. Archive 25, Robert Opie 26 (b), 27, Bodleian Library 32 (a), Benelux
Press/Ace 32 (b), Fotopic/Ace 33 (a), Roger-Viollet 33 (b), Gary Crallé/Image
Bank 34 (a), Pictor 34 (b), Visual Arts Library 41, Peter Newark's American
Pictures 50, Visual Arts Library 56, Thierry Perrin/Rex Features 52 (a), 53 (a
& b), Colman's of Norwich 58 (a), Mount Horeb Mustard Museum 58 (b),
Bridgeman Art Library 71, Harry Smith Horticultural Collection 83 (b), e.t.
Archive 91, Bridgeman Art Library 105, 119, Mount Horeb Mustard Museum
97, Robert Opie 99, Colman's of Norwich 100–101, Robert Opie 112, Robert
Opie 113 (a), Thierry Perrin/Rex Features 113 (b), Robert Opie 114 (a),
Thierry Perrin/Rex Features 114.
All other photographs are the copyright of Quarto Publishing plc.
Quarto would also like to thank Chris Wilson at Colman's of Norwich for all
his help and Elizabeth David Cookshop, The Piazza, Covent Garden, London
EC2E 8RA for supplying equipment for photography.

Author's Acknowledgements (KH)
My thanks go to Tim, my chief taster, for tasting every recipe in the book,
some several times. I would also like to thank Theresa and Ray for their
endless trips to my kitchen and honest opinions. Thanks also to my sister
Emma for helping out when deadlines loomed, and to all my other willing
tasters, including Sue, Tony and Tina.